Helping Faculty Find
Work-Life Balance

Helping Faculty Find Work-Life Balance

The Path Toward Family-Friendly Institutions

Maike Ingrid Philipsen
Timothy B. Bostic
Foreword by Mary Ann Mason

JOSSEY-BASS
A Wiley Imprint
www.josseybass.com

Published by Jossey-Bass
A Wiley Imprint
989 Market Street, San Francisco, CA 94103-1741—www.josseybass.com

Readers should be aware that Internet Web sites offered as citations and/or sources for
further information may have changed or disappeared between the time this was written
and when it is read.

Limit of Liability/Disclaimer of Warranty: While the publisher and author have used their
best efforts in preparing this book, they make no representations or warranties with respect
to the accuracy or completeness of the contents of this book and specifically disclaim any
implied warranties of merchantability or fitness for a particular purpose. No warranty may
be created or extended by sales representatives or written sales materials. The advice and
strategies contained herein may not be suitable for your situation. You should consult
with a professional where appropriate. Neither the publisher nor author shall be liable for
any loss of profit or any other commercial damages, including but not limited to special,
incidental, consequential, or other damages.

Jossey-Bass books and products are available through most bookstores. To contact Jossey-Bass
directly call our Customer Care Department within the U.S. at 800-956-7739, outside the
U.S. at 317-572-3986, or fax 317-572-4002.

Jossey-Bass also publishes its books in a variety of electronic formats. Some content that
appears in print may not be available in electronic books.

Library of Congress Cataloging-in-Publication Data
Philipsen, Maike.
   Helping faculty find work-life balance : the path toward family-friendly institutions /
Maike Ingrid Philipsen, Timothy B. Bostic ; foreword by Mary Ann Mason.
      p. cm.
   Includes bibliographical references and index.
   ISBN 978-0-470-54095-4 (hardback)
   1. College teachers—Professional relationships—United States.   2. College teachers—
Family relationships—United States.   3. College teachers—Job satisfaction—United
States.   I. Bostic, Timothy.   II. Title.
   LB1778.2.P45 2010
   378.1'2—dc22
                                                                        2010023124

The Jossey-Bass
Higher and Adult Education Series

Contents

To Rosie, Lucy, and Morris, who masterfully balance work and life.

Foreword

Achieving work-family balance has been a hot item on the agenda of most colleges and universities for the past few years, but for the most part the initiatives have been put forth by women and the recommended solutions are for women. Men are often left out of the discussion and the solutions because they are not considered to have a problem. They rarely complain about family balance and they seem to be doing just fine in their careers.

Philipsen and Bostic make it clear that this mother-centric line of thinking is out of date. Today's partners share parenting tasks. The men in Generation X, born between 1965 and 1985, most often do take on their fair share of domestic responsibilities, unlike their fathers before them, and they need institutional support just as mothers do.

Through careful interviews of both men and women (the "men's study" and the "women's study"), Philipsen and Bostic unpack the complicated feelings that today's parents have about struggling to provide equitable support for their partner while still maintaining a confident, uncomplaining manner. These interviews are conducted at early, middle, and late career stages, acknowledging that achieving life-career balance is not just a problem for early parenthood.

In addition to these valuable insights of the faculty members, much of the book is a careful analysis of what five different types of "traditional institutions" are offering: two public comprehensive universities, a flagship university, a private comprehensive university, a community college, and two historically black colleges—followed by a description of six "exemplary institutions." Together these chapters provide a great compendium of the range of family support systems available nationally, and some of the problems and pitfalls that many of these programs have confronted. These chapters will serve as a great resource as institutions of higher education continue their efforts to make universities more life friendly—for both men and women.

Mary Ann Mason
Professor and Codirector
Berkeley Law Center on Health,
Economic, and Family Security

Acknowledgments

First and foremost, we thank the participants in these studies, the faculty members who generously gave of their time to be interviewed and to read the transcripts, as well as the informants who provided us with background information about the work-life policies on their campuses. We thank our own institutions, Old Dominion University and Virginia Commonwealth University, for supporting this project in the form of grants, research, and clerical assistance. Thank you to the staff at Jossey-Bass for their professional support.

Our families and friends have, once again, been superbly supportive, and we thank Jon Wergin for repeated and careful editing, Tony London for his unwavering support, and Niklas, Sven, Morris, Lucy, and Rosie for cheering us up.

The Authors

Maike Ingrid Philipsen has been employed since 1993 at Virginia Commonwealth University, where she currently holds the position of professor in the social foundations of education. Born and raised in Germany and educated in Germany, the United States, and Canada, Dr. Philipsen came to Richmond after receiving her Ph.D. in social foundations at the University of North Carolina at Chapel Hill. She had previously earned her master's degree in political science at the Free University of Berlin.

Dr. Philipsen's research interests center on issues of social justice and equality in education, specifically the roles of race, gender, and social class in shaping schools and institutions of higher learning. She studies questions relating to equal opportunities at both the K–12 and college/university levels, employing primarily a sociological perspective and qualitative methodologies. She teaches students at all levels ranging from undergraduate to doctoral studies and is the lead faculty member at the university's PFF (Preparing Future Faculty) program.

Timothy B. Bostic has been employed at Old Dominion University (ODU) since completing his Ph.D. in 2006 at Virginia Commonwealth University. He earned an M.A. in humanities, focusing on feminist theater and English literature at Old Dominion University, received his postbaccalaureate certificate in education from Virginia Wesleyan, and taught high school English in

Norfolk for six years. He also has a B.B.A. in finance from George Washington University and a B.A. in speech communication and theater arts.

After spending almost six years in an urban high school class-room, he decided to get his Ph.D. in education in order to work on creating more equitable learning environments for all students. He has conducted quantitative studies on barriers to males entering the teaching profession, the impact of teacher empathy on standardized test scores, mobility's effect on elementary school achievement, and evaluation of an ESL curriculum implementation for adult learners. He also researches effective practices for teaching writing. He was the director of composition for the Department of English at ODU, where he taught future secondary English teachers how to teach writing. After spending a year as a research scientist in The Center for Education Partnerships in the Darden College of Education at ODU, he is now an assistant professor of English education in the Department of English at ODU.

Introduction

Highly accomplished at midcareer, as full professor and department chair at a prestigious research university, Dr. Dennison has reached the conclusion that his family is "not coping." His sixty-one-year-old colleague Professor Rabinowitz looks back and says: "There were times in my career when I simply gave up a personal life." And Assistant Professor Moller, a productive scholar with a bright future, sums up her feelings: "I would be hard-pressed to name more than a handful of people in my field total who have thriving personal lives outside of the field."

Such testimony is alarming, and a system of higher education that prides itself on leading the world can and must do better. Some institutions have begun the journey to increased life-friendliness, and, as this book shows, much can be done even in times of budget cuts and economic stagnation.

The faculty is the backbone of any college or university, and can be neither healthy nor productive if not cared for in ways that allow for a successful balance of personal and professional lives. Taking the institutional perspective, considerable resources have typically been invested in the hiring of new faculty, and losing talent because of work-life issues is economically detrimental. As Clark and d'Ambrosio (2005) caution, "universities must develop compensation policies and employment practices that are appropriate for the new economic and demographic environments"

(p. 386). When we asked her about the financial implications of a life-friendly workplace, Provost Sullivan at the University of Michigan replied, "It is a savings in the long run because faculty think well of Michigan and their time here. We want to foster loyalty, and it increases loyalty. It gives you an institutional strength that you can't get any other way."

Given the important role that faculty play in an institution's success, we decided to make public what faculty have to say about their work-life relationships. We give voice to their stories about how they experience major issues related to life-work balance. These issues include crafting a career, having partners, parenting, and seeking to thrive against all odds. We depict what is and what could be, describing enablers and obstacles encountered at the institutions where the participants worked, and how policies and programs might more effectively address their needs. What happens when policy meets faculty?

Interwoven in our depiction of faculty members' realities as they see it, then, are the results of our search for institutions that have made efforts to meet faculty (and often staff and student) needs in balancing work and life. We use a constant comparative approach in showcasing the challenges that faculty face, the enablers and coping strategies they employ to thrive to the extent that they do, and what can be learned from exemplary institutions working to address the needs of faculty.

This book emerged from two consecutive studies: one on the challenges female faculty face trying to balance their personal and professional lives (Philipsen, 2008), henceforth called "the women's study," and a second on male faculty, henceforth called "the men's study." Based on the finding that men are beginning to encounter obstacles similar to those facing their female colleagues, we decided to extend our research even further and include what academic institutions can do to make a faculty career attractive to all professors. Though we report challenges unique to academic women, we also show how work-life issues are, less now than ever before, simply "women's issues." They, instead, affect faculty across gender lines and therefore both male and female faculty benefit from progressive institutional programs and policies.

In this work we are heeding the call to write a "narrative of faculty growth"—and what it takes to achieve it—in addition to what has been called a "narrative of constraint" (O'Meara, Terosky, & Neumann, 2008, p. 2), meaning portrayals of faculty primarily as struggling within challenging circumstances. Although there is no denying that our research on both male and female faculty unearthed many constraints, and those will not be omitted from our accounts, we also found both individual coping strategies employed by faculty and institutional programs and policies geared at enabling faculty growth. It is our intent to render these two accounts—of constraint and of growth—for the dual purpose of understanding more fully the former and thereby strengthening the latter.

Research indicates that beginning scholars of both genders are increasingly seeking work environments that permit them to effectively address both their personal and professional responsibilities (Rice, Sorcinelli, & Austin, 2000). Doctoral students note the constant pressure and stress in their teachers' and advisors' work, leaving some to wonder whether a balanced life is possible or whether they should rethink their career goals (Austin, 2002). Therefore, as Austin writes, it is imperative to take action and improve the quality of academic work life, given that it is not merely a personal but an institutional issue (Austin, 2006, p. xiii). Along similar lines, Mason, Goulden, and Frasch (2009) found that especially research universities are at risk of losing some of their best talent because many doctoral students are looking for careers that allow well-balanced lives. Institutions of higher education, particularly fast-track research universities, have a bad reputation in that regard, and they may soon face a pipeline problem when young scholars opt out of faculty careers and look for alternatives. Change is therefore necessary. And because the "concrete lived experience is a key place from which to build knowledge and ferment social change" (Hesse-Biber, 2007, p. 3), we attempted to better understand the lived experiences of faculty balancing acts alongside the social change that is currently taking place in some colleges and universities.

Though still a relatively new research focus, work has been done recently on work-life balance in academe (Drago & Colbeck, 2003; Mason & Goulden, 2002; Mason & Goulden, 2004; Williams, 2000), and some of it is beginning to focus on specific recommendations for best family-friendly practices (Gappa, Austin, & Trice, 2007; Quinn & Shapiro, 2009). What makes our approach unique, however, is its comparative approach not only in regard to gender but also in regard to career stage. Whereas most other work-life literature either focuses exclusively on, or at least emphasizes, the challenges facing junior faculty, with the occasional discussion of elder-care issues for late-career faculty, we designed both studies to include experiences of male and female faculty at early, middle, and late career stages. This approach allowed us to compare and contrast challenges to work-life balancing that are more prevalent, if not unique, to some generations when compared to others. And though much of the literature on work-life balancing seems to be written with an eye on the needs of female faculty, especially female faculty with children, we deliberately broadened our view and studied, in-depth, the perspectives of male faculty also. In addition, rather than falling into either the "restraint" or "growth" approaches explained above, we sought to apply both lenses and report equally on challenges and enablers of work-life balancing. Finally, though "family-friendly" has become a household term in academe, it is our belief that we need to go beyond and make institutions of higher education "life-friendly," thus addressing the balancing needs of faculty without families at home as well. Therefore, we deliberately diversified our samples and included participants of various family constellations and sexual preferences, allowing us to look at ways in which work-life balancing challenges not just academics who have children at home.

Not only did we talk to a diverse group of faculty, but we also selected diverse institutions to showcase (more detail about their characteristics in Appendix A: Methods and in Resource A: Exemplary Institutions). They include public, private, research intensive, elite, liberal arts, comprehensive universities and a community college. We did not exclusively focus on wealthy institutions either, who can afford to spend on programs and policies to meet faculty needs, but also on those that are just as strapped for resources as the majority of American universities and colleges currently are. In addition, we made a conscious effort to highlight policies and programs that do not cost much or, in some cases, are even cost-neutral. It was our intent to highlight what can be done without much financial wherewithal, based simply on ingenuity and innovative thinking. After all, this book's purpose would be seriously curtailed if it were relevant solely to institutions with money.

Organization of the Book

This book is organized by theme; the first three chapters discuss one of the major issues that faculty in both the women's and men's study reported as challenging: crafting a career given the typical attributes of tenure-track positions in most colleges and universities (Chapter One); establishing and maintaining partnerships (Chapter Two); and parenting (Chapter Three). Each of these chapters combines faculty testimony given the realities of their institutions, recent research on the issues, what kinds of policies and programs might help in their situations, and what exemplary institutions offer specifically to address the topic. Each chapter ends with recommendations specific to the topic.

Chapter Four focuses on faculty thriving. Also based on the women's and men's studies, it weaves together stories about factors that enable faculty and help them fare as well as they do, trying to balance work and life. It includes testimony about people, policies, programs, and individual coping strategies.

Chapter Five summarizes main findings, draws conclusions, and not only provides a succinct summary of recommendations as made throughout the book but introduces additional recommendations addressing issues larger than those discussed previously.

One unique feature of this book is its extensive provision of resources in the appendix. In Resource A, we list the policies and programs that exemplary institutions offer and URLs that link to additional information. In Resource B, we provide a user-friendly guide to information about child care, spousal/partner hiring, child leave, and flexible tenure policies. Resource C provides additional useful resources, readings, and organizations.

In Appendix A, we discuss the methods used in both the women's and men's studies. We describe the participants, data collection, analysis, and the settings that employed the participants as well as those that served as exemplary institutions.

Finally, in Appendix B, we include additional parts of the men's study. The information goes above and beyond those topics that constitute the main body of the book, such as crafting a career and the need for flexibility (Chapter One), partnering (Chapter Two), parenting (Chapter Three), and thriving (Chapter Four). Nevertheless, we concluded that it was important to share some crucial insights for those who would like to learn more about our conversations with men of different generations about work-life balancing. We take a bird's-eye view of how men talked about work-life questions and make comparisons to how the women sounded, speculating what might be learned about gendered discourses and constructions of masculinity. Another issue we problematize is that although even today, in comparison with many women, many men continue to enjoy advantages, it would not be accurate to omit the dark sides of privilege that men experience. We will, therefore, introduce their stories about costs and sacrifices such as pressure and the provider syndrome. We also give voice to other issues they addressed, image and ego, and how those affect the central question of this study, the balancing of personal and professional lives.

Helping Faculty Find
Work-Life Balance

1

Crafting a Career

Both male and female faculty participants consistently refer to significant changes over the course of their career spans and across generations, at work and at home—significant enough to be a turning of the tide. At work, these changes pertain to faculty workload, roles, and rewards, and though they are seen as affecting junior faculty members most dramatically, senior faculty feel them too. At home, role definitions and divisions of labor are changing, again more so in junior faculty members' lives but not without impact on their senior colleagues. None of the institutions that employ the participants in our studies, however, have kept up with any of these developments. Instead, they remain steeped in old models of how faculty work and live. Expectations, especially pertaining to scholarly productivity, have risen significantly while the time frame within which to achieve tenure has not been adjusted. Faculty members of both genders tend to carry significant responsibilities in their personal lives, but they are still expected to function "as if they had wives at home." Women face a system in which the pre-tenure years often coincide with their last childbearing years, and yet the tenure structure remains rigid. Over the career span, faculty of both genders continue to be challenged to fulfill their roles not only at work but also at home, often adding the care of aging and ailing parents to their responsibilities later in life, and yet workload adjustments hardly exist. Based on stories told by participants at various stages in their careers, the following sections illustrate the need for change, particularly for increased flexibility in defining individual workload and career paths. Emphasis is put on the pre-tenure phase because the urgency for flexibility is most pronounced then.

Although the institutions represented in our studies had little to offer in terms of career flexibility, others do. First we make the case for increased flexibility, and then introduce several exemplary institutions that have taken seriously the call to meet faculty needs and have instituted policies and programs accordingly.

The Increase of Expectations

The earliest years in a faculty member's career life cycle are likely to be the most difficult ones (Olsen & Sorcinelli, 1992). Our data suggest that this is still true, and one primary reason lies in the particularly high expectations during the probationary period. While nontenure-track and part-time appointments are rising, thus rendering the tenure system less relevant to increasing numbers of academics (Schuster & Finkelstein, 2006), many are still affected by the pressure characteristic of the pre-tenure existence. According to our participants, this pressure affects work-life balancing.

"Am I able to balance . . . ? I would say 'No. Not at all,'" are the words of Dr. Moller, an assistant professor who is convinced that what she sees as her rather limited success at establishing a healthy balance between the personal and professional spheres of her life is symptomatic of the academic profession. It is not just she, in other words, who is struggling at finding balance but such struggle comes with being a faculty member in a high-pressure environment. Not being able to find a satisfying balance is, furthermore, not exclusively an issue for faculty with families but is typical of most faculty members, and affects men as well as women. In her words:

> In terms of personal life, family is just one aspect of personal life. I would be hard-pressed to name more than a handful of people in my field total who have thriving

personal lives outside of the field, because there's just so much pressure in general on performing academically that there isn't much room left for personal life. . . . I was told early on when I was a grad student by one of the senior faculty in my department that I could have at best two of the following three things. I could have a career, a life, or a family but you can't have all three. I found even having two was hard, but I can't do all three successfully. Even for the men, you can barely do two successfully.

Indeed, a male assistant professor in his third year reports that it is "a huge challenge to have any kind of personal life and do what you're supposed to do," and a first-year historian characterizes his personal life as having been "swallowed up" by his professional life.

While participants in both studies acknowledge that pressures exist at all career stages, they agree that new generations of faculty are especially hard hit, and one central concern is the increasing emphasis on scholarly productivity and research output. Students of higher education have long criticized the "corporatization of the university" and how institutions of higher education increasingly define "expertise and the reward system in terms of scholarly rather than pedagogical expertise" (Glazer-Raymo, 1999, p. 202). Finkelstein, Seal, and Schuster (1998) found more than a decade ago that new faculty (defined as full-time with up to seven years of experience) emphasize research productivity to a greater extent than senior faculty (defined as full-time with seven or more years of experience). More recently, they confirmed the mounting importance of research expectations over time (Schuster & Finkelstein, 2006). These tendencies resonate with Assistant Professor Williams, who is convinced that the younger generation is required to produce, if not more output in general, certainly more research than previous ones; and this produces tension in his department at a liberal arts college that seeks to polish its national standing. The older generation does not believe the college ought to emphasize research over teaching, whereas the younger generation resents having to carry a disproportionately large part of the research burden, and refers to the senior generation as "dead weight."

Others attest to the drastic increase in pre-tenure expectations. Assistant Professor Selinski, for example, believes that the amount of time he has to put into his professional labors is far greater than what most of his predecessors did. "I think they were less encumbered with paperwork, with politically correct nonsense, with compensating for the failures of the students. For one, the students were better trained," he claims. Previous generations, according to him, were under less pressure to publish and had more time for family and outside pursuits than his generation.

It is not just junior faculty who assess the changes in academic requirements in this way: many of their senior colleagues agree. Dr. Jarman, who has served his institution for more than thirty years, says that formerly the standards were not as high as they are nowadays. His college used to primarily be a teaching institution whereas now things are a lot more difficult for young faculty: "They're putting in a lot more time than I think I did in terms of pursuing their scholarship, particularly in the . . . probationary period."

Professor Lewis, who is in his thirty-fourth year, simply says: "There were no formal tenure requirements when I started." Senior Professor Ingrahm agrees: "I just submitted a file to the dean. And ultimately the tenure showed up. So I wasn't particularly aware of what happened to the process after I submitted this file. And then I had the tenure." Professor Jellig remembers how thirty years ago putting in time was all it took to get tenured and promoted. Beyond that, "there was not anything that you had to prove that you had done one thousand and one publications and that sort of thing."

Compounding institutional expectations, junior faculty nowadays "tend to sort of get sucked into doing some things they probably don't have to do," according to Senior Professor Jarman. He observes at his private liberal arts college an emphasis on personal and interactive relationships with students, one-on-one work in addition to the usual research and classroom responsibilities. Some of his colleagues take this obligation too seriously, he thinks: they do independent research with too many students and advise too many of them. "Sometimes my younger colleagues in order to make sure that they either get tenure, or that they get a good salary, or that they get promoted, whatever . . . tend to go overboard in trying to meet expectations. I think there are ways that my younger colleagues could cut back on their working here in order to achieve that healthy balance."

Senior Professor Sneed locates the responsibility within the institution rather than the individual. He has great sympathy for his junior colleagues and does not endorse the current institutional trend of inflationary expectations. "I think it sucks," he says. "I think we're still really schizophrenic here. . . . I think that the demands we make on junior faculty include a good balance, and that it is reprehensible that we do not go out of our way to make their lives better. . . . I think there's a lot of bullshit that we ask people to do that we don't need to do for the sake of the status quo."

Increased scholarly requirements do not exclusively affect junior faculty, of course. Senior Professor Ashcroft describes his own institution as becoming more research oriented, an effort he believes is unrealistic given the higher teaching load it continues to face. "The teaching load that we have, you don't have over at Johns Hopkins," he says. Yet the trend of growing research expectations remains.

Although those expectations may affect faculty across the board, regardless of stage and status, one junior professor suggests that tenure is what makes the difference in workload, and once tenure has been obtained, chances are better to create a reasonable split between personal and professional pursuits. "I can only go by what

I've observed with senior researchers," says Dr. Ruggerio, assistant professor of nursing. "They have a lot more time on their hands to deal with family life and to have more of a social life."

There is an overall consensus among faculty across the career span, in short, that senior professors are better positioned than their junior colleagues to successfully balance their lives. This assertion was borne out by the study on women faculty which found that whereas participants at midcareer continue to struggle with balancing issues, most late-career faculty report a very healthy balance between their personal and professional lives. But again, that is not true for junior faculty, and the problem of rising expectations is compounded by the fact that these expectations tend to lack clarity.

Lacking Clarity and the Paradox of Flexibility

Cathy Trower researched generational differences in academe and found that "Generation X" scholars have a "new view" of academic employment policy that is markedly different from the "traditional view." Younger scholars want clarity of the tenure process, criteria, and standards, as well as the evidence required. They demand clarity of expectations for scholarship, teaching, advising, colleagueship, and campus citizenship and, in addition, they are asking for reasonable and consistent performance expectations, as well as consistency of messages from senior faculty and administrators (Trower, 2005, p. 17). Yet what they want is still far removed from what actually exists at least at the seven institutions we included in our study.

There, unclear expectations often make life difficult for beginning academics, a problem well-defined by existing literature (Colbeck, 2006). It has been argued, furthermore, that nebulous criteria and processes for tenure, promotion, and merit increase academe's potential for bias against caregiving in academe (Drago & Colbeck, 2003). If and when faculty do not know what expectations they need to meet professionally, in other words, it is difficult for them to openly and diligently pursue personal obligations. In short, unclear expectations at work directly affect faculty's personal lives. And despite efforts in many places to make especially tenure expectations more transparent, in the institutions we studied they had largely remained unclear.

Assistant Professor Moller calls tenure expectations a "moving target," elaborating that one of her biggest struggles derives from feeling that nothing ever gets done to the extent or with the quality she would like. Academics, she explains, tend never to know how much work is enough and, subsequently, carry a constant sense of guilt because they are never doing as much as they could. The academy is remiss at providing clear expectations, and as long as faculty do not know what, exactly, the expectations are and what it takes to succeed, they are doomed to try to do as much as they possibly can, often sacrificing obligations to self and others.

Coupled with the problem of ill-defined expectations is the paradox of flexibility. It appears that academics have too much of it and, simultaneously, not enough. According to Healy (quoted in Gappa, Austin, & Trice, 2007, p. 240), "[f]lexibility is a way of defining how, when, and what work is accomplished, and how careers are organized." In some ways, faculty members enjoy a relatively high degree of freedom to define the boundaries between their personal and professional lives. If and when coupled with unclear expectations, however, such freedom is not always experienced as helpful. Assistant Professor Dr. Calhoun, for example, explains her inability to enjoy flexibility:

> Part of the problem for me at least is that when you don't have a clearly defined nine to five job it is not like you can leave at the end of the say and say "I'm done." Your project is always with you in a certain sense. On the one hand, I feel like I have a lot of free time because my time is not scheduled. On the other hand, I feel

like I don't have any free time because since my time
isn't scheduled, or as scheduled, at any moment I could
be working or arguably should be working. Sometime
I think if I could set banker's hours in some way and sort
of tell myself that I'm working from eight to six and
then I'm done, but thus far I haven't had a lot of success
holding myself to those commitments.

Along similar lines, Colbeck observes that faculty may have
much discretion over how they allocate their time and integrate
roles, but they work under intense pressure to meet high expectations that are often unclear. She quotes a colleague saying
that faculty "enjoy the freedom to work themselves to death"
(Colbeck, 2006, p. 47).

The issue of flexibility is even more complex given that faculty
members' relative autonomy in organizing daily routines stands in
stark contrast to the rigidity that characterizes their work in other
respects. Gappa, Austin, and Trice (2007, p. 240) make a similar distinction and argue that the concept of flexibility ought to
recognize individuals' responsibilities beyond the workplace, thus
allowing for major adjustments of work schedules such as leave
taking or shifting from full-time to part-time work. In addition,
it "encompasses providing career-path options, such as multiple
points of entry, exit, and re-entry into a faculty position, and
the ability to shift between tenure-track and contract-renewable
appointments" (p. 240).

And yet, faculty members, especially junior faculty on the tenure track, tend to have little flexibility, if broadly defined. Not
only do they lack opportunities to make significant schedule and
career adjustments, they are typically bound by a career path that
demands their undivided attention for at least five consecutive
years before they are eligible to be tenured. And though senior
faculty members may be able to apply for sabbaticals or research
and study leaves, some institutions do not grant such options to

their junior faculty. Out of the seven institutions represented in our study, for example, six offered sabbaticals to their faculty but only two extended the offer to its nontenured faculty, an ironic reality given the rise in expectations particularly for that group.

Flexibility, in short, is more than simply *not* having to punch a time clock, fill out time-sheets, or otherwise account for every working hour of the day. It is a concept that, if "integrated into the culture and policies of an institution," allows faculty members "to negotiate work arrangements that reflect the current level of their personal responsibilities" (Gappa, Austin, & Trice, 2007, p. 241). Our studies of both male and female faculty members at various institutions indicate that we are far from making these kinds of provisions.

Women on the tenure track often experience most poignantly how lacking flexibility has the potential to curtail faculty aspirations. As illustrated in the women's study and documented elsewhere (Mason & Goulden, 2004, 2002; Mason, Goulden, & Wolfinger, 2006), the pre-tenure years often coincide with women's last childbearing years. They are up against both their tenure and biological clocks. And because the pressure of the tenure track makes it difficult to have children and simultaneously work as full-time faculty members, women find themselves in a position where they have to make a choice between having children and pursuing their career, seemingly unable to do both. The following quote by Assistant Professor Calhoun captures the dilemma:

> The thing I worry about the most in terms of this question about balance is the . . . whole biological clock problem which is that my pre-tenure years are also, for whatever reason, in sync with the years in which I should probably, if I want to have a child, I should be doing it. I will get tenure provided everything goes all right when I'm 38. According to a lot of doctors that is getting late to start a family. I haven't found a way to

start a family yet while on the tenure track. The one thing that would make a difference to me is if there was a way to make tenure sort of not coincide with one's child producing time. It isn't that I don't want to get tenure. Obviously I do. It would be nice if tenure didn't have to be such a rigid thing. As it stands, I don't feel like I can really prioritize finding a partner and getting pregnant right now. So, I have to sort of roll the dice on whether or not I will ever be able to carry children. Which scares me. To get a more flexible schedule for tenure would make a big difference, I think.

Female faculty on the tenure track are asked to make choices their male counterparts hardly ever have to make, namely the choice between family and work. Not surprisingly, research illustrates that women who enter the tenure track without children have less than one in three odds of ever having children. In addition, a majority of men (60 percent) are married with children twelve years after receipt of their Ph.D. whereas only a minority (41 percent) of women on the tenure track are married with children (Mason, Goulden, & Wolfinger, 2006, p. 16).

Though men fare better in the long run, partly because they do have the option to postpone family formation until after tenure, our research on male faculty found that the pressure of obtaining tenure acts as a major stressor for them as well, and since many male junior faculty also begin their careers at an age at which family formation occurs, they find, at best, a tenuous balance between their work-life responsibilities. Because of these stressors, many believe they will get married and have children after tenure, a course of action highly recommended by their mid- and late-career male colleagues. Such a delay, though perhaps not desirable, is at least possible for men. As mentioned previously, women typically do not have the same biological luxury. Instead, they may have to engage in what Drago & Colbeck call "productive bias avoidance," meaning behaviors such as delaying childbirth intended to shield them from negative consequences they may face if and when they have to take care of others in addition to pursuing their careers. Such behavior is productive in the sense that it prevents sacrificing one's career; in fact, it may improve work performance. Drago and Colbeck argue that women more frequently employ such avoidance behavior than men, leading to "disparaging outcomes": men and women face identical performance standards but women are forced to pay a higher price to meet them (Drago & Colbeck, 2003, p. 4). For Dr. Calhoun, the price is possibly forfeiting motherhood.

Although her male colleagues do not face equally dramatic choices, our research indicates that men are beginning to struggle with the incompatibility between academe and personal commit-ments. And though it is not always easy to balance life for those male faculty who have partners and families, as the following chapters will discuss, being single creates its own challenges. Dr. Trenton points out: "The . . . scenario I have seen with male academics is that if you don't have family already, it might be hard to start one once you are in these positions because the ten-ure thing is so over your head that no one feels like they have vast amounts of time to go out and find a partner." He mentions his brother, also an academic, who only started investing more time in dating after he got tenure. "He really just forgot about that while he was doing his book and trying to get tenure," says Dr. Trenton. About a friend in a similar situation he says: "I don't know what to say to him because I know he would like to have a family but also he's not going to commit professional suicide to earn that."

Our study found a paucity of single men. Of the forty-one men interviewed, only three were single, and one was divorced without having remarried. In comparison to female faculty, these numbers indicate that the vast majority of male faculty are in committed relationships, whether with a significant other or a wife. However, the experiences of the men who had remained single were fasci-nating and bear recounting.

The pre-tenure single men are clearly putting their personal lives on hold while they take the time to establish their careers. When asked whether he has a healthy balance between his personal and professional lives, Professor Ruggerio says: "There could probably be a lot more social life, but you know, just because of the time restraints within the tenure track, it doesn't really allow much time for that." In response to the same question, Professor Hall presents a similar scenario: "My professional life is sort of swallowing my personal life, but I am assuming that's only temporary. I don't know . . . I don't feel like I have enough downtime this semester." Both express hope that their life balances will improve as their careers develop. Professor Ruggerio, speaking about his life after tenure, says, "I'm hoping I can see some kind of, at least a 50/50 split." Professor Hall feels that things will settle down, and "maybe I can start looking more seriously [for a significant other] in a bit." Both share the belief that they will eventually be able to have more fulfilling personal lives. However, midcareer Professor Price indicates that the length of time he has been single may cause problems should he be able to find a life partner. He says, "I don't regret my long bachelorhood, but it [a relationship] is something I want to have. . . . If I were to find the right person and get married, which I think would be good, I recognize that I'll have some challenges because of how long I've lived on my own." Thinking about friends who have been married since they were young, he muses: "I know a couple of people who got married, and he was 20 and she was 19, and they're still married, and it's a very happy marriage, and they know each other in a way that anybody I marry now will never know me. When they see this person, they see this long arc of what this person was like as practically a teenager and through early adulthood and then maturation. For some people that might be disastrous, for this couple that seems to be a really comforting thing. I know I will never have that now, you know."

Those men who choose to have children pre-tenure are often forced to pay a price as well, as the following chapters illustrate in detail. It is clear, then, just how urgent it has become for institutions to create tenure policies that do not disadvantage women or men who have children before obtaining tenure.

In summary, higher education, faculty roles, rewards, and the definitions of what it means to be a successful academic have undergone considerable changes over the last decades, some of which carry important ramifications for faculty members' abilities to balance their lives. Participants in both studies observed the mounting importance of research expectations over time, a trend most significantly affecting pre-tenure faculty. They, in turn, perceive themselves as carrying undue burdens in comparison with senior colleagues. Given that productivity standards across other realms of academic work have been ratcheted up as well, most junior faculty end up with less time to spend on personal pursuits than their senior colleagues. The tendency is ironic, however, as it is typically the earlier years in a career during which people build partnerships and families; they do it at a time when they can least afford it.

For many reasons, institutions need to offer more flexible workloads and career plans. Junior faculty may desire the option to have more time available than five years to get ready for tenure, either because they face increased productivity expectations or for reasons related to their personal responsibilities. Women, for instance, may want to break out of the rigid five-year system to be able to start a family without being forced to give up their careers. Mid- and late-career faculty, in addition, may have to reduce their workload to deal with family or health-related crises, elder care, and a myriad of other issues.

At the seven institutions included in our studies, none had the kind of flexibility that allowed faculty at different career stages to custom-tailor their work schedule so that they would be able to respond to personal needs. No institution allowed for part-time tenure-track work options or for reentry to the tenure track after prolonged absences. Stoppage of the tenure clock, if available, was negotiated individually with department chairs or deans, and extended leaves for personal reasons were either not available or, again, individually negotiated and taken as "research leave." Yet some institutions are more progressive, and we will now take a look at what can be done to allow for faculty flexibility, with an emphasis on flexibility in the design of the tenure track.

Exemplary Institutions

University of Washington

Though quite a few institutions allow faculty to extend the probationary period for various reasons, usually related to pregnancy, childbirth, and adoption, the University of Washington exceeds those provisions and offers an array of flexible work arrangement options for both faculty and staff. According to Quinn and Shapiro (2009), because time is such a scarce resource, flexible work arrangements (FWAs) are a top indicator of work-life quality and employee satisfaction. They note that FWAs are becoming increasingly necessary given the increase of caregivers in academe and, furthermore, they typically involve only minimal costs.

For one, UW offers its faculty the so-called stopping of the tenure clock. The Academic Human Resources website reads: "The University recognizes that under special circumstances, such as care for new infants, faculty women and men must devote extraordinary efforts to their family responsibilities which may significantly detract from their research and academic capabilities. Even if the faculty member continues to work full time, efforts normally devoted to scholarship may necessarily be reduced by these new family responsibilities. In recognition of these family obligations, the University has developed several programs to stop temporarily the tenure clock" (University of Washington, n.d-b). If a faculty member takes a medical or family leave of six months or more, he or she is automatically entitled to an extension of the pre-tenure period. But even without taking a leave, or if taking a leave shorter than six months, a faculty member is entitled to a tenure clock extension if "family care responsibilities have interrupted the regular dedication to teaching or scholarship" (University of Washington, n.d.-b) as long as it is requested prior to the year of review.

According to Quinn and Shapiro (2009), a 2007 study showed about 25 percent of tenure-track faculty making use of the extension policy with more women than men using it for personal reasons, and more men than women for professional reasons. Stopping the tenure clock has had no effect on the attainment of tenure, and almost all faculty who used the policy were glad they had done so. The authors recommend the following to those who wish to replicate the policy:

1. To counter the perception that the policy accommodates, and inadvertently stigmatizes, women, it ought to be structured in such a way that faculty of both genders are eligible to use it.

2. To avoid a "mommy-track" and increase inclusiveness, reasons other than childbirth ought to be included such as caring for family members, personal medical reasons, or professional reasons such as loss of lab space.

3. Because some faculty may realize they need an extension years after the triggering event, they ought to be allowed to ask for it then.

4. To help change the perception that usage of the policy is "abnormal," department chairs should be encouraged to discuss it regularly at annual review times. (Quinn & Shapiro, 2009)

Beyond the stoppage of the tenure clock, a faculty member at UW can decide to choose among several part-time tenure track options. Specifically, he or she may be initially appointed for the duration of three years at 50 percent or greater of full-time responsibilities. If the appointment is renewed, the second appointment allows the faculty member to choose to work at 90 percent or more of the full-time load for three years, 70–89 percent for four years, 60–69 percent for five years, or 50–59 percent for the duration of six years. At the end of the second probationary period, whatever its length, the faculty member will be reviewed for tenure and promotion. Provided it is in the written agreement by the dean of the assistant professor's school or college, the faculty member may, at any time, change the percentage and terms of the appointment, as long as they are consistent with the numbers just mentioned (University of Washington, 2002).

The part-time tenure track option was introduced at UW in 1998, and initially few faculty members made use of it, according to Quinn and Shapiro (2009), partly because it proved difficult to define and evaluate a part-time research agenda. They report that most of those who did go part-time, furthermore, were post-tenure but that recently the number of pre-tenure faculty using part-time options has increased, particularly among women in science and engineering. Faculty report appreciation for being able to spend time with young children or aging parents, or, for late-career faculty, to ease into retirement. Quinn and Shapiro have the following advice for those who wish to replicate the policy:

1. Expectations need to be defined in writing and shared with tenure review committee members.

2. Departmental teaching obligations need to be met when a faculty member goes part-time without overburdening other department members. Since part-time options saves salary dollars, this money can be used to cover those obligations.

University of Michigan

Michigan does allow for a stoppage of the tenure clock, available to both women and men. This option is open to "a faculty member who must help meet the demands of caring for dependents" (University of Michigan, 2005a). However, as has been noted by Jaschick (2009), stopping the tenure clock often comes with concomitant problems. External reviewers and tenure committees may look at the length of time a person has been in probationary status and judge the amount of scholarship produced as insufficient, given the "extra year." Commenting on Jaschick's article, Janice Bellace, a former associate provost at the University of Pennsylvania, believes that other institutions should do what Penn has done, which is to inform external reviewers that a child care extension had been taken by the person being evaluated (Jaschik, 2009). Further, tenure committee members also need to be educated about this policy. According to UM's provost and vice president for academic affairs Dr. Sullivan, "we are going to need to move to a longer tenure clock." She also believes that "colleges and schools [within the university should] vote on whether they want to lengthen their tenure period. We don't need a one-size-fits-all policy." This type of flexibility promoted by a senior administrator helps to ensure that the policy is being used because faculty are given the message that it will not have a deleterious effect on their careers.

University of California at Berkeley and Los Angeles

Both campuses allow for stopping the tenure clock, and both campuses have an eight-year probationary period. To make sure faculty understand the policies and programs tied to faculty work-life issues, UCLA, through its office of Faculty Diversity and Development, provides information that is easily downloaded. The brochure gives the pertinent websites and the links to relevant policies. It provides the four key points about tenure stoppage for faculty who are in their eight-year probationary period. "Childbearing or parental leave of one quarter and up to one year will be excluded from service. The tenure clock may be stopped for up to one year for each event of birth (or adoption or foster care) up to a two year limit. . . . Requests for time off the tenure clock must be made within two years of a birth or adoption. Stopping the tenure clock should not disadvantage faculty in promotion, advancement or compensation. The file must be evaluated without prejudice, as if the work were done in a normal period of service" (University of California, 2003c). The policy is very clear. However, long-term faculty member Dr. Miller at UCLA admits that "the culture does not predispose people to utilize policies," so whether faculty are taking advantage of the policy is difficult to discern. The policy at Berkeley is the same; they have gone further to ensure that the policy is communicated, however. Nevertheless, Dr. Mary Ann Mason, UC Berkeley law professor and codirector of the Center for Economic and Family Security, points to the communication issue: "It's a constant effort to make clear what the policies are. On our campus, it [stopping the tenure clock] is a default option. You automatically get the tenure clock stopped unless you don't want it. This is a much fairer system." The benefit of this "default" option is that a faculty member has to ask *not* to stop the clock rather than to stop it; therefore, no one is made to feel as if he or she is the beneficiary of a special accommodation. Again, stopping the tenure clock for a new child is a relatively common practice in institutions of higher education. Its use, however, seems to be limited because of the fears faculty have about possible repercussions. Berkeley has removed that fear, and thus has made good on its promise to be family friendly.

Williams College

Interestingly, the tenure stoppage policy at Williams is not as progressive as some of the institutions we studied and definitely not as progressive as our exemplary institutions. Faculty members who wish to obtain a one-year delay in a tenure decision need to have taken "more than one parental leave prior to a tenure decision" (Williams College, 2009). This policy requires a faculty member, then, to have had two children before stopping the tenure clock.

Thus, the implicit expectation is that junior faculty continue their scholarship while taking a semester of paid parental leave.

Faculty member Dr. Alonzo (pseudonym) mentioned another program at Williams that could be seen as an aid to work-life balancing. Williams has a Mortgage Program and "makes subsidized mortgages available to eligible faculty and administrative staff in order to assist them in acquiring homes in the Williamstown area. This benefit is intended to help these employees when first entering the Williamstown area housing market" (Williams College, 2009). The program offers loans at half the posted interest rate of one of the local banks. Dr. Alonzo explains that "because the institution wanted faculty to stick around and be on campus, they felt that faculty needed help buying houses in Williamstown." Despite the high cost of real estate surrounding the college, junior faculty are encouraged to purchase homes near campus.

In response to the question of how well work-life policies and programs are communicated, Dr. Alonzo explains that although the institutional mission is "good, there is not much commitment to doing something when departments are reluctant to change." According to her, administrators usually come from and go back to the ranks of the faculty which both helps and hinders. On the one hand, Williams does not have the kind of antagonistic relationships between administrators and faculty as many other institutions. Instead, the administration is very faculty-friendly. On the other hand, because the bulk of the senior administrative staff does not consist of professional administrators, "there are problems when it comes to getting them to recognize where Williams is behind the curve." There is, according to her, a tendency to think we are Number One, we've always done it this way, why change?

Still, from Dr. Alonzo's perspective, Williams is making concerted efforts to address work-life issues in a proactive way despite resistance emanating especially from some of the older faculty.

Boise State University

Boise State University allows for a one-year extension of the tenure clock under certain circumstances, including the birth or adoption of a child. Multiple extension requests may be granted. The institution's policy states explicitly that

> If a probationary period extension is approved, a reduction in scholarly productivity during the period of time addressed in the request should not prejudice a subsequent contract renewal decision. Any faculty member in probationary status more than the standard four (4) or five (5) years because of extensions shall be evaluated as if the faculty member has been on probationary status for the standard four (4) or five (5) years. (Boise State University, 2009, p. 7)

Boise State University recently received an Alfred P. Sloan Award for faculty career flexibility and, in addition to developing a mentoring program and successful policy communication structure, the institution is currently working on the development of part-time tenure-track options for its faculty. Such arrangements would add another layer of flexibility to faculty members seeking to expand their options and be better able to balance work-life responsibilities.

When asked about obstacles on the road to policy implementation, Provost Andrews and Academic Affairs Director of Professional Development Anson reiterated familiar themes: the importance of communication, for instance. "You just can't communicate enough," we were told. At the start of every semester Boise State sends all faculty a list of the career flexibility policies and procedures websites. Boise State also encourages departments to provide information on its career flexibility programs early on in a person's career at the institution, namely in the acknowledgment of his or her job application package. In addition, the provost meets with every department in the process of faculty hiring, talking about policies and encouraging the department to communicate the availability of these policies and programs to applicants. These steps are meant to alleviate fear potential hires may have about inquiring about family-friendly policies. They don't have to bring up the topic; it is done for them.

Another roadblock facing family-friendly policies can be tradition. Faculty are trained to value individualism but the flexible workload policy, for instance, is based on people having to think like a family. "It's like doing Saturday chores," explained Dr. Andrews. "Not everyone can mow the lawn; someone has to take out the trash. There are all these things that need to be done, and we need to divide them up. Departments need to be receptive to functioning as units rather than as individuals. Here at Boise State, we have rewarded with new resources departments that demonstrate commitment to moving as units."

San Bernardino Valley College

San Bernardino Valley College does provide tenure to its faculty. The CTA Bargaining Agreement requires faculty to be evaluated "during the fall semester of the fourth year of service" (San Bernardino Community College District, 2010a, p. 54). Though the agreement does not specifically spell out that the tenure clock can be stopped, faculty member Dr. Jiminez (pseudonym) explains that "tenure is granted after the successful completion of four fall evaluation cycles. If for some reason, you were off for the entire fall or spring, it would mean that you have another year." Issues surrounding scholarly productivity are not relevant because faculty are evaluated on "expertise in subject matter . . . techniques of instruction . . . effectiveness of communication . . . [and] acceptance of responsibility" (San Bernardino Community College District, 2010a, pp. 50–51). Therefore, though faculty's tenure would be delayed for one year if they took time off, there are no penalties for doing so.

Policy Meets Faculty

Relating what is available at exemplary institutions back to our interview data, one cannot help but imagine how much happier and productive Dr. Moller, who believes she had to choose among a career, a life, and a family, would be if she had supportive policy options. Knowing that she could opt for a flexible work arrangement, such as that available at the University of Washington, without damage to her career might increase her quality of life and, by extension, her employment satisfaction. Providing flexibility would, furthermore, be cost-effective for her institution given that adjuncts to cover her classes are less expensive than paying her at a full-time rate. It is also likely that a diminishing stress level would positively affect her productivity as a scholar.

Further, working hard to make all members of a promotion and tenure committee aware that junior faculty members' materials are to be evaluated on a standard of four or five years, as Boise State or Berkeley do, gives teeth to otherwise ineffective tenure clock stoppage policies. Being assured of fair and uniform evaluation criteria, regardless of whether faculty take time out to deal with various life circumstances, would help junior faculty realize that their institution understands they have a life outside of work. It certainly would make a difference for someone like Dr. Trenton. It seems eminently distressing to think he feels that trying to work on building a relationship and starting a family amounts to career suicide. By creating and effectively communicating life-friendly policies to all parties involved, academic institutions might create happier and more productive faculty whose institutional commitment would be cemented, making them less likely to leave an institution that has made considerable investments in them.

Faculty need clearly outlined tenure expectations. Our data indicate that in few cases were clear tenure goals communicated to pre-tenure faculty. This uncertainty ramped up expectations for the faculty we talked to and, by extension, left them unnecessarily stressed. Perhaps senior faculty within a department would be more prone to help their junior colleagues by crafting clear expectations for tenure if departments were rewarded for acting as a unit, a successful practice engaged by Boise State. Had such clarity been established at his college, Professor Sneed might not see his junior colleagues going "overboard in trying to meet expectations." Creating a cultural shift away from traditions of individualism toward collective visions and practice, however, takes time. Organizing informal brown bag sessions such as the ones at Michigan and routinely meeting with departments engaged in faculty hiring as practiced by the provost at Boise State are promising first steps. In the following section, we make further policy recommendations relevant to the issues discussed.

Recommendations

Rigid tenure schedules are confining in that they do not allow the flexibility necessary to deal with major life events. Therefore we recommend that:

- Stopping the tenure clock in case of childbirth or adoption becomes a default option, as at the University of California, Berkeley. As a result, tenure clock stoppage becomes the norm rather than the exception and thus loses its potentially stigmatizing character.

- The institution ensures that department chairs, external reviewers, and tenure and promotion committee members are well aware of the details pertaining to tenure clock stoppage to avoid the common pitfalls of the policy, namely the expectation of increased productivity when a faculty member was given "an extra year."

- Schools and departments individually consider whether or not to lengthen the probationary period, given that a university does "not need a one-size-fits-all approach," in the words of Michigan's Provost Sullivan.

- Tenure extensions be granted for reasons other than childbirth, such as caring for family members or for medical reasons. Doing so would address equity concerns by making all faculty, including those without new children, eligible for extensions. In addition, it would avoid the creation of "mommy tracks."

- Flexible work arrangements be introduced, such as those provided by the University of Washington. These are low-cost options with significant positive impacts on work-life balancing efforts.

- Part-time options for tenure-track faculty be provided. An excellent example is the University of Washington, which allows faculty to choose among several different part-time scenarios.

2

Making It Work: Having Life Partners

Numerous studies address the benefits and stresses that come from being partnered in academia (Astin & Milem, 1997; Jacobs & Gerson, 2001; Jacobs & Winslow, 2004; Norrell & Norrell, 1996). Many of the male and female faculty we interviewed believe that their partners have been immensely enabling to them as a support system. Unfortunately, those whose life partners are also academics face a unique situation when they enter the job market. Miller-Loessi and Henderson (1997) point out that the changing nature of society has "radically altered the professoriate in a number of ways, including dramatically increasing the number of couples" [sic] (p. 25). Drago and Colbeck (2003) suggest that faculty are often forced to choose between family and employment goals because existing societal forces make it difficult to achieve in both realms. However, many try.

Being partnered generally proves helpful for most academics, regardless of gender, yet it tends to necessitate all kinds of negotiations, among them how best to divvy up household chores. And our research indicates that though many men would like to believe that they are contributing 50 percent to household duties, for the most part women still end up doing a larger share of the work. To shed light on dual-career couples' coping strategies, we will look at how they divide up home responsibilities and how they manage. We are joining the chorus of those who have argued before us that because of the increase in academic couples, higher education institutions need policies to address the dual-career issue. At the end of the chapter we discuss the policies existing at the institutions where our research was conducted and then detail policies at institutions that illustrate forward thinking on this issue.

Division of Labor

"Thus was the turf; there was the path," writes Virginia Woolf about her encounter with a man who makes it clear that she, a woman, does not belong among scholars (Woolf, 1929/1999, p. 258). The participants in the men's study also tell tales of rigid gender-based divisions of labor, still true for many of those in active employment today. They state what is well known, namely that late-career men, as their predecessors, tended to be the families' sole breadwinners with stay-at-home wives and thus, as one participant puts it, they "didn't have those problems with the homemaking side to worry about." Even more so than today, a man's identity used to derive from "what he did," according to Professor Sneed, and a professor had a wife who was, in Professor Price's words, "an assistant to his career." Public and domestic spheres were largely separated, as illustrated by late-career Professor Ingrahm. He recalls his post-doc times at a major research university where the philosophy department threw parties not inviting wives "because it would lower the tone." A faculty wives club existed, and members were called "the bibelots." "It sounds rude," he says, "but it was actually a word that means 'an ornament' or 'a useless ornament.'"

Thankfully, as a society, we have made strides to correct such prejudices. Jacobs and Winslow (2004), listing many of the "firsts" women have achieved since 1973, argue that regardless of the numerous equity issues women still face, it is important to remember how much improvement has actually occurred. It was, however, this type of rigid gender division that provided men with the domestic support structure necessary to fulfill their role as an "ideal worker" (Drago & Colbeck, 2003; Gappa, Austin, & Trice, 2007).

As many male academics have partners who are also academics, it is no wonder that the stress level derived from tensions between work and home demands has increased in recent years (Jacobs & Winslow, 2004). The "ideal worker" relies on an old model of family structure that no longer exists. Most faculty have a working spouse or life partner, so there is no one home who could create an environment that allows either partner to devote all of her time and energy to an employer. According to the 2000 U.S. Census, 37 percent of all families in the United States consisted of dual earner couples. As this number continues to rise, higher education institutions, like many of their corporate counterparts, must begin to address this reality if they are going to be able to recruit and retain productive faculty.

Listening to the men at the middle and late career stages, it becomes clear just how much has changed. They recount how academe used to be largely a male-dominated world, and domestic duties were exclusively part of the female domain. "I never saw my Dad cook," says Mr. Holmes at Community College, a man in his forties. "I never saw my Dad wash any clothes, I never saw my Dad clean the house. He just didn't do that stuff. . . . He was a long-distance truck driver . . . and he worked and made the money and [my mother] paid the bills and kept the house and made sure we did what we had to do as children. So it was pretty clear-cut then." His mother taught him domestic skills, however, and those came in handy when he found himself a single parent later in life.

Other men talk about changing times as well, and how they were affected by transitions from clear-cut divisions of labor to more participatory models. This shift helps explain why 74 percent of the next generation of male scholars are concerned about how family-friendly their potential institution is (Mason, Goulden, & Frasch, 2009). Dr. Zavella at HBCU is an immigrant from Peru who grew up in a traditional household and tried to hide from his father how he had changed.

See, I couldn't be like my father who would just come home to the house, drop his briefcase, sit, grab a beer, not even grab a beer, go 'Honey, get me a beer.' I got home from school, and if my wife was still at school, I would just fix something for the girls. . . . I don't think I would have been able to do this back where I come from because I remember washing dishes, and the phone rang, and I picked up, and I was talking to my father, and my father said: 'What's that in the background? Do I hear water running?' And I said: 'Oh, I'm washing the car, Dad.' I would never admit to my father that I was washing the dishes. We grew up with maids. And if the maids were not there . . . then my sisters and my mother would take care of it. . . . It was very patriarchal. . . . I changed diapers. . . . A lot of men my age, even now in my country, wouldn't do that.

In comparison, female post-doc Dr. Carver believes her husband does a lot of the domestic chores, a situation that leads to a more even division of labor than most couples experience, something that she describes as "incredibly enabling" to her career. Women's participation in the labor force has increased significantly over the last fifty years, more so among white women than among women of color and immigrant women who, for various reasons, were less free to stay out of the labor market (Kramer, 2005, p. 133). The trend for women's economic behavior to increasingly resemble men's is expected to continue (Hartmann, 2004, p. 229). Younger men nowadays more typically encounter two-earner situations, and though it seemed "normal," in Assistant Professor Trenton's words, for women of his mother's generation to stay home, he would now "feel appalled if I let my wife stop work because she gets so much out of it and . . . what she's doing is so important for its own sake." Among his colleagues, he reports, it is a pretty standard assumption that your partner is going to be doing something. "It's just a different set of cultural norms. . . . It's so far out of my conception to think that I'd go home at 6:00 P.M., and there's going to be dinner waiting for me. We have never organized it like that. Never in my wildest imagination would I have a spouse who would do all these services for me, and I think that way was the norm thirty years ago."

Questions of how to divide labor are not just to be negotiated in terms of employment; they are waiting at home too. Most early-career male faculty believe that they shoulder a relatively equal amount of household responsibilities, and yet, even among younger faculty examples can be found of men who acknowledge their wives' busy careers, but who nevertheless do not handle their fair share of domestic duties. Some participants hold on to the deeply ingrained idea of the "superwoman," and though they admit that their wives are busy professionals, they appear to think there is something intrinsically amazing about women that allows them to do everything. This is, for instance, how Dr. Ionesco sees his wife: "She's a remarkable person. She gets up at 4:30 every morning; I don't know how she does it, but she cooks, she cleans, she's able to get her lesson plans done. So she really holds it down to hold the house together."

Displayed here is a so-called negative advantage (McIntosh, 2000), meaning a blindly accepted advantage that reinforces hierarchical social realities. Author Steven Schacht provides examples for such negative advantages that he, as a man, enjoys. He writes, "If I am married or even cohabiting, I can count on my wife doing most of the housework and being responsible for most of the childcare, should we have children, regardless of whether she works or not" (Schacht, 2004, p. 27). Though the continuing existence of unequal distributions of labor shall not be denied, there are nevertheless indications that early-career faculty men tend to work toward more equitable arrangements. This fact is supported by early-career faculty member Dr. Nelson, who credits both her extended family and her husband with being her main supporters.

Her husband makes sure, she explains, that she is being left alone so she can get her work done, and he is the one to whom she can turn for advice. Her experience supports the idea that, for some, being partnered makes it possible to balance both realms.

The ways in which faculty divide labor suggest that gender is not always the deciding factor. Some, for example, split chores based on personal preference rather than unbending beliefs about men's and women's work. Professor Mahoney, an early-career faculty member, points out that he and his significant other "have the complete gender swap. . . . And my happiness has increased realizing that this is true. I do the shopping and the cooking. . . . She cuts the grass in the summer, she does all the mechanical, electrical . . . all the stuff that involves tools or any kind of mechanical knowledge or something like that." It is obvious that younger men are no longer rigidly controlled by gender norms in terms of what they can or cannot do. Professor Mahoney, as many others, "always had this ideal of egalitarian relationships," and could not quite imagine not performing domestic work as equal partners.

Even in families with more traditional arrangements, men tend to acknowledge their wives' preoccupation with their careers. Many negotiate ways to divide things up so that no one is overwhelmed. Early-career Professor Landers describes the "deal":

> We have something in our household where we say can you handle it today. And what that basically means is that it is not a good day, I need you to take my back on this, and so generally the other person will take the person's back. If, for instance, I come home and my wife says can you handle it today, that says to me honey, can you cook dinner, can you watch the kids the rest of the night because it's been one of those days. And sometimes I say that. But we don't have a clear distinction at all.

Professor Allison knows that his wife "is the kind of person who, if she feels like things are not [equitable] she lets me know." His colleague Professor Johnson points out that he and his wife alternate their schedules so that "her classes will be in the morning . . . so I can work from home. . . . If something does come up at school where we need to get the kids or anything, I'll be there. . . . So it will just be a nice trade-off." Thus, many early-career faculty share the understanding that both partners in the relationship must be willing to pick up the slack when needed.

The trends described here confirm what was found in the women's study (Philipsen, 2008): the distribution of domestic labor has shifted over time. The so-called double shift, with women being expected to perform all household and child care–related duties in addition to their careers is waning, it was argued. Early-career faculty member Ehrenreich believes that women of previous generations had so much more pressure to fulfill all responsibilities at home, in addition to their jobs. She says she hopes that women of current generations are more likely to have spouses or partners who see household labor as the responsibility of everyone who lives in the house, instead of the woman's job alone.

According to end-of-career faculty Saltmarsh, women of younger generations are indeed more assertive and demand more of their partners in terms of participation in domestic duties. She says: "I think women today . . . from the beginning, they expect more from their spouses. I think women today want more time for themselves." Their attitudes contrast with the ones prevalent among her and previous generations, which she summarizes as: "If I'm going to work, I still have to do everything else."

Although distinct generational differences exist, the view of partnership models as superior to more conventional ones is not restricted to early-career faculty. Midcareer Professor Molina at Community College calls the image of the male professor cooped up in his study while a supportive wife is raising the kids "sad" and, if the image is true, a "loss for that generation." He says,

"Men were not operating on all cylinders for a hundred and fifty years of American culture," and though he admits that he may be projecting, he thinks that previous generations of men would have wanted to spend more time at home than their work culture allowed them to.

Midcareer men in our study generally personify a triad of themes concerning the division of labor in their homes. Some expect to take an active role in domestic affairs; they report that work is divided pretty evenly and in sync with their view of relationships as partnerships. Professor Eggleston says that he did "not expect the model of the '50s wife. . . . I never longed for my wife being at home, even though it would have made my life a little easier, probably." This thought is echoed by Dr. Zavella, an immigrant scholar from Peru. His highly educated wife was unable to work but she found staying at home highly unsettling; so he helped her find volunteer work at his institution. Eventually, "they saw so much potential in her that they made her a research assistant, and they gave her a full ride to do her master's." Professor Dotolo and his spouse made a conscious effort to raise their children together, "both exploring it together . . . [and] it still makes me feel . . . it's a good thing [that] I was right there from the start."

The second theme among male midcareer faculty is the belief that they are sharing equally in domestic duties while they acknowledge evidence to the contrary. Professor Sneed remarks that he was very active in raising his children, yet he concedes that "it would be interesting to hear this from my wife's perspective." His "life was simple because basically child rearing was something I did when I chose to, rather than something that I *had* to do" (emphasis added). Professor Ashcroft is married for the second time and believes he is doing much better this time around because he is taking a more active role, ensuring that his spouse is not the only one who carries all home and child-rearing responsibilities. However, when something goes awry with the schedule, his spouse bears the brunt of the work: "When the child gets sick, we had two children, and they get sick, it was almost understood, which I feel guilty about, but [she is] the one who is going to stay home because I have all of this to do. I may only have one or two classes a day, but you know, I'm doing other things." So even though he assumes he is taking on an equal load, he admits that when crises occur, it is his spouse who deals with them—alone.

The third theme to emerge among midcareer men around the topic of labor divisions were rationalizations for why they did not take on a fair share of domestic work. As Dr. Jankovich, a professor at Public Comprehensive University, relates:

> I didn't get involved in [school issues] because she recognized the fact that since I was the one bringing home the paycheck that it was more important for me to stay where I was and not be involved in the day to day things that go on with the kids as far as during the school day. But when I got home from work and after we had dinner, then we were pretty much open to do what we wanted to do. . . . And that's pretty much how it was when I was a kid, too. My family functioned basically the same way.

Along similar lines, Dr. Collado and his partner created a domestic partnership agreement in the mid-1990s, spelling out a clear division of labor. Because his partner was "very intent on having a very ordered home," and, in addition, had a job less lucrative or satisfying than Dr. Collado's, the partner took on most of the domestic duties in the couple's home. Likewise, Dr. Hanson believes that "whoever is the more prominent wage earner needs to go out and do that, and whoever is not would tend to take care of the other things." His assessment stems from being "an economics major; so I tend to view things through an economic lens." This rationalization is shared by Dr. McDaniels, who insists that he does vacuum and help with the laundry, but his "wife still does most of that [help with school work, cook, and so forth]. And thank God, I love her for that. I know she's tired when she gets home sometimes, and she still cooks, and she does what she has to do, it's become routine." He believes that she wants to do these things, and the kids want her to do them, so he does not see why anything should change.

At the late-career stage about half of the men approaching retirement believe that they and their partners attempted to make an even split of their personal responsibilities. However, there is an acknowledgment that things did not always work out that way. Some late-career faculty experienced a change over time, how-ever, and report that they are currently doing more at home than before, perhaps even finding the tables turned. Dr. Lewis calls it interesting that now he is "the one keeping the home. . . . Our roles have changed, and it worked out well." Dr. Ingrahm says he and his wife "tried to take the 50-50 approach, but I think more fell on her. But also, she was more eager to undertake mom sort of things . . . so I figured that wasn't necessarily undercutting the 50-50." Dr. Jellig, however, thinks of himself as a "forerun-ner of Mr. Mom, and I had a ball." Dr. Richards describes how he and his wife "had some division of labor, and some areas of specialty that I did that she didn't do and vice versa. We tried to keep it balanced." The men felt they were equal partners in their relationships.

However, the other half of the late-career faculty experienced a different world given that their wives stayed at home, at least when the children were young. Though it is clear that most of the participants cherish their relationships, it is equally apparent that many did not think much about issues surrounding their spouses' careers, and some remain downright dismissive of them and their work. Late-career Professor Jillian's wife has a master's degree in his field, and they met while working on a project together before he obtained his doctorate. She quit her professional career to take care of household and children but then, as he puts it, "she got a little bored with whatever she was doing which was housewifing, and she decided to . . . [have] sort of a second career in retail." The professor interprets this new path as nothing more but her attempt to catch up with him who, after all, had meanwhile earned a doctorate. He states, "But at the master's level, at least, we were equal, and I think that was our biggest problem. She never voiced it, but I think that's what her problem was. Now I would be superior to her, and she's the kind of broad that has to feel that she's in charge. . . . Broad? That's a term for 'woman.'"

Other late-career faculty members display different sensibilities. Sixty-six-year-old Dr. Green at Private Comprehensive, for instance, compares his generation with that of his sons, and unequivocally voices his admiration for the way they negotiate work, family, and partnerships. "All four of my sons are very sensitive . . . are considerate to their girlfriends and have made very good boyfriends and husbands, in one case. . . . I see all four of my sons as much more considerate than I was at that time. In fact, I've learned that from them. So it's kind of an interesting situation. I see, in a way, what would have been a better way to accomplish these relationships, these balances, than I did in my own life."

He calls his sons "much more enlightened than I was as far as parenting is concerned," and tells the story of his oldest, married with four children himself. He and his wife struck a perfect balance; they took time with their kids and, even at the expense of their professions, made the family life work. Dr. Green recounts how his son ". . . talked about various other people he went to medical school with, how they were single-mindedly ambitious and looking for the best internships and striving for these particular placements and earning a lot of money. And I must say he didn't appear to be driven by those same kinds of ambitions." His son's wife got a master's degree but somehow the two of them still found the time to homeschool their children. The professor calls the stresses on his son's family "recipes for disaster" but admires how they master taxing situations. He attributes the junior's success to realizing the value of family and, together with his wife, curbing professional aspirations. "I just marvel," he concludes, and relates that his son is not much different from the younger generation of male faculty members at his college. "They seem to be more concerned for others than themselves," he says. "I see them more sensitive to gender issues than I ever was."

Not all senior faculty judge generational changes as positive, let alone enviable. Instead they are longing for the good old days. Sixty-seven-year-old Professor Jackson fondly remembers his parents' and his own generation, and perceives his son's plight as a "very bad situation" in comparison. These are his words: "The man went off to work, and all the work was done, at home, by the lady. That's the model [my wife and I] had, that's the way it worked in both families. . . . Her father had never in fact seen the inside of a kitchen until he was a teenager when he snuck in to find out what went on in there."

Times have changed, and Dr. Jackson's son, who is an academic himself married to another academic, and father of a fifteen-month-old child, is in a very different situation than his father was. "My son seems to be chief cook and bottle washer, seems to be in charge of everything except the actual physical nursing of the child. . . . The wife is an academic, perhaps not completely successful. . . . I see [my son] doing—trying to do—his academic work but always spending time and money securing time for her to do hers; and I would say that's a very bad situation. But that's because I'm spoiled by the situation I had myself, which was lots and lots of hours to do my work without anyone bothering me."

In sum, though male faculty in all three career stages displayed some similarities, overall their differences are stark. Early-career men, by and large, view their relationships as partnerships with equals, and they divide work accordingly. They expect to do their fair share of domestic duties, want to be equal partners, and are willing to negotiate responsibilities which they do not see as determined by gender. Midcareer men find themselves caught in the middle between two competing beliefs. On the one hand, they see their younger colleagues taking on an equal amount of responsibility for home and child care. On the other, they see many of their older colleagues enjoying the luxury of a stay-at-home wife. The men in this group seem to either be in line with their younger colleagues and their values or aligned with their older colleagues who, even if their wives did not stay at home, allowed the bulk of the housework to fall on them.

End-of-career faculty found themselves as part of the generation who had the tide of expectations turn on them. Some embraced new ideas about equality of labor; some did not. Many of those who did seem to have found contentment in their wives' desires to pursue the careers for which they had prepared, and they worked to provide the support necessary for that to happen. This, in turn, proved lucky for those who came behind them and now have role models to help them understand what is expected of them and how to balance their personal and professional lives.

Dual Careers

Aptly, Wolf-Wendel, Twombly, and Rice (2003) titled their book about dual-career couples in the academy *The Two-Body Problem*. The job market for academics is typically a national one, and newly hired faculty may have to move long distances. Given the scarcity of jobs in many disciplines, and the selectiveness involved especially in awarding tenure-track positions, couples may indeed face a "two-body problem," particularly if the so-called trailing partner is also an academic. Regardless of the institutional affiliation of the men or women in our studies, the challenge inherent in two academics looking for work was prevalent. Fortunately, a number of institutions are beginning to acknowledge this reality.

Not surprisingly, we found that early-career faculty typically decided where to go based on who received the first job offer.

Considering that in the United States 35 percent of male faculty and 40 percent of female faculty are coupled with another academic, negotiating dual careers is becoming an increasingly important issue (Astin & Milem, 1997). Though it is possible to understand from a theoretical perspective the stressors for dual-career academics, their stories bring to life the trauma that many experience.

Given that many of the men at early and midpoints of their careers have partners who work outside the home, they needed to learn to manage their personal and professional responsibilities accordingly. They had to make compromises in order for both people in the relationship to be able to pursue a career. Professor Ampofo and his wife, for example, face the challenges typical of scholars in similar fields. They were married in graduate school, and because he was the first to find a job after completing his dissertation, his wife moved with him to a small university. However, due to the rural nature of the location, her employment opportunities were limited. The couple decided to look for work in a geographical area home to several institutions of higher education and, indeed, both secured tenure-track positions. However, they now live about one hour from his campus and about twenty minutes from hers. They only partly solved the dual-body problem: their situation created problems that, as he put it, require "constant negotiations."

Dr. Allison and his wife are both in the same department at a public comprehensive university. As the institution has no spousal/partner hire policy, he initially followed her to the area and taught as a lecturer at a university nearby. After her second year, he was able to obtain a tenure-track position in her department. He believes that their "situation worked out well" but is quick to point out that they have "been lucky in terms of . . . two people who are in academe" because he knows "lots of people where it was not easy finding jobs in the same area." Dr. Mahoney at the same institution, for instance, is well aware of his career limitations because of the "two-body problem." He did not apply for a position at a more prestigious institution because his significant other would have been unable to find work. Looking back at previous generations, he concludes, "That is the kind of thing I could have done if it were a traditional arrangement. But you know you can't do that when you have a partner."

It seems that only in few instances are both partners able to craft the kind of situation described by Dr. Allison. For most, managing two careers creates the need for compromise. Junior Professor Daughtrey worked out a job-sharing deal that allowed him to enter the tenure track. His wife had received tenure at the university before he obtained the job. He believes the institution's desire to keep his wife happy motivated it to find a solution to the couple's dilemma. The arrangement caused him to feel a moral obligation not to fail: "People have to realize that every situation is different, that there isn't a one size fits all, and everybody has to be open to creative solutions, and it all depends on the place that you're at, too. There are a lot of places still that would never contemplate doing this type of arrangement. If I feel pressure, it's in that respect. I feel like I have to make this work; otherwise, I'll be sort of closing the book on people in the future."

Midcareer Professor Eggleston highlights the need for academic couples to make compromises. He and his wife went on the job market determined to entertain offers only from institutions ready to hire both of them. "We were down to four schools that were willing to make offers to both of us. And so we really eliminated every other option. But each of us probably could have had a more prominent position if they didn't consider the offers available to the other one." Dr. Molina at Community College knows that because his wife did not take on progressively more demanding positions when their children were small, she wants the opportunity to do so now. He finds himself agreeable to her desire to take an administrative role that requires him to shoulder more of the domestic responsibilities and thinks they "might end up doing that back and forth over the next several years. . . . I think that works really well." Clearly, he is willing to make the requisite concessions to enable his wife to "have her turn" in crafting the career she desires.

Unfortunately, even if both partners are open to compromise their careers in some ways, logistical problems may well increase the stress of dual-career academics trying to balance their personal and professional responsibilities. Dr. Dennison serves as an example. For a while he commuted from his place of employment on the East Coast to the Midwest where his wife had a faculty appointment. When the strain became too great, she found a position on the East Coast, but it is still a four-hour commute from his institution. He knows that the "set of conflicts that we clearly resolved in one way [were not resolved] without consequences." It caused his wife to get "quite depressed about where her professional life has taken her," and the compromise has left both feeling either professionally or personally frustrated. Because his wife's appointment is in a city so far away, she now stays gone for part of the week, rendering Dr. Dennison the single father of their five-year-old twins. He feels tremendously stressed and, in his own words, "vulnerable." His marriage is slipping, and it has much to do with the extreme strains that the commuter and dual-career couple faces. In order to get everything done, Dr. Dennison gets up at 4:00 A.M., and so he goes to bed right after he puts his children down. "That means I do absolutely nothing at night," he says. "That's a coping strategy; it also has painful consequences." His wife does not share his schedule, and so "we're sort of crossing paths. Times for intimacy and times for exchanging information and thoughts and stuff are harder to come by because of my schedule. So it's coping in one sense, but the opposite in another."

Though these kinds of problems are more common nowadays, they did exist in the past. The women's study uncovered a harrowing story of a dual-career couple and the human cost it exacted because institutions were not concerned. Seventy-five-year-old chemistry Professor Amici has spent fifty years as a scholar in her field. Her native country is Italy, where she received her Ph.D. at age twenty-five. She worked in places that were at the top of her field at the time, such as Oxford University and the University of Milano. In 1960, she met an American scientist at an international conference. They got married, and she emigrated to the United States in 1961, where her husband had a university appointment. She was thirty-one years old. "At that time, there were no women in [my field] in the United States," Dr. Amici says. "There were some in Europe, because Europe was about 20 to 25 years ahead of the United States in so-called women's rights." She was completely ignored, she recalls, and yet she wanted to keep working. So for 14 years she worked as an unpaid post-doctorate at her husband's institution, doing research and helping him. She worked essentially full-time, she says, but she did not have an academic appointment. The couple wrote books together that gained national recognition, but she was never granted a position at the university. When their youngest child was about two years old, Dr. Amici's husband intervened. She remembers:

> My husband said if you wait any longer, it will be too late for you to start a career again. So, he said, I will spread the word, because he was very well known, that I will move if they give you a position. So he was willing to give up his very well established situation so that I could get a chance. He did get offered an endowed chair at a university, and they offered me a position as a full professor, because I was qualified. Even though I had stopped working, I had papers published and books written.

Considering the stress associated with dual-career academics and their quest for receptive institutions, it is not surprising that a number of publications address this issue (Ferber & Loeb, 1997; Gappa, Austin, & Trice, 2007; Norrell & Norrell, 1996; Wolf-Wendel,

Twombly, & Rice, 2003). The need for policies that help support dual-career couples is clear, yet at the institutions where both of our studies were conducted, the absence of any effective policies was striking.

Regarding spousal/partner hiring, Public Comprehensive's faculty handbook states that "the vice-president of the search for which the spouse is an external candidate is allowed to request of the president of the university that the spouse be hired." It is emphasized that funding for the position must be made available, and that consultation with the dean, provost, faculty, department chair, and so on have to occur before an informal offer may be made. Despite the policy's existence on paper, however, interviews revealed that no one on campus seemed aware of it. Process and policy are in place, but they do not seem to be communicated to people instrumental in the implementation process.

Metropolitan makes mention of spousal hiring in its guide to recruiting diverse faculty. However, the onus is placed on the search committee, which is encouraged to locate available campus resources and even set up job interviews. As a caveat, the guide informs search committee members that they do not need to broach the subject if the candidate does not bring it up. Thus, although both institutions are aware of the needs of dual-career couples, neither has a codified system for handling them.

Flagship University has no spousal/partner hiring policy that is obtainable. A spousal employment link exists on the website, but when clicked, nothing appears on the screen but an error page. Private Comprehensive does not have a spousal/partner hire policy. In an in-house publication about Private Comprehensive's policy, the interim provost stated that the institution tries "to help when we hire a faculty member who has a 'trailing spouse.'" In the case of the two HBCUs and Community College, the policy search turned into a depressing enterprise. No spousal/partner hiring information was to be found. Fortunately, there are institutions that possess more effective policies geared at alleviating the two-body problem. It is to the exemplary institutions that we now turn.

Exemplary Institutions

University of Washington

Dr. Quinn, the project director at Balance@UW, emphasized that the high cost of living in Seattle makes it difficult to make ends meet with one salary, a reality that partly explains her institution's dual-career policy. Although the university shies away from promising positions to partners and spouses, the institution commits to doing "all we can do to help." In the sciences, in particular, she says, chairs have a network and do work together to accommodate partners and spouses. She calls the Higher Education Recruitment Consortium (HERC) "amazing" but points out that UW is not part of it. All that can be found in regard to spousal/partner hiring on the university's website is the statement that UW has responded to the emergence of dual-career partners by "informally providing job assistance services to the partners of new employees" (University of Washington, n.d.-a). Even so, over the years, many academic couples have been accommodated. In 2004, for example, twenty-two such accommodations were arranged.

University of Michigan

The University of Michigan takes a very proactive stance to ensure that they attract the best possible faculty and provides resources and assistance to make sure they stay. According to Provost Sullivan, hiring committees do not get involved in considering how to accommodate life partners and spouses, but once the decision is made to extend a job offer, "we want this issue to be taken up." Michigan, understanding that "dual career partner assistance [is] a crucial element in recruiting and retaining its excellent faculty," has both a policy on dual-career hires and a "Dual Career Program." The mission of this program is described as follows:

> Many faculty members recruited by the University of Michigan have partners who are accomplished professionals in their own right. The ability of your spouse or partner to find a suitable career opportunity may be a key factor in your decision. In response, we have created the Dual Career Program. As a prospective or new faculty member, be sure to talk with the chair of the search committee, the department head, or the dean about the Program. (University of Michigan, 2007)

The University provides a downloadable guide for prospective faculty members and their partners. When asked whether or not this program is effectively communicated to faculty, Dr. Sullivan replies that if deans and department chairs "don't know about it, they haven't been listening." Understanding that a tough economic environment might not make it possible for the University to be able to offer a position to a spouse or life partner, UM has created a Higher Education Recruitment Consortium because, again in the words of Dr. Sullivan, the university "knows [they] may not have a position for a spouse, but [they] may be able to find one at a nearby school."

In order to ensure that administrators at Michigan understand the program, a document outlines the spousal hiring process as well as administrative roles and responsibilities. Michigan not only assists partners and spouses in finding academic positions, but they also provide links to major employers in the area. The University of Michigan aids new and prospective hires though helpful hints, brochures, and resources available through the office of Recruiting and Employment resources, making sure that new faculty understand that Michigan's commitment to dual-career couples is not simply talk. Considerable efforts are being made to help spouses and partners find gainful and appropriate employment.

University of California at Berkeley and Los Angeles

The University of California (UC) actively handles this problem as well. Although none of the UC institutions guarantee jobs to partners, the 2003 "President's Summit on Faculty Gender Equity" addresses the dual-career issue. One recommendation reads:

> Because women faculty are more likely than men to be part of dual academic career couples, the University of California should develop model programs for dual career hiring. Such programs could include centers to promote faculty spouse/partner employment opportunities, centralized campus-wide funding to support spouse/partner hiring, and participation in regional college and university consortiums to pool academic employment opportunities. (University of California, 2003a)

Both UCLA and UC Berkeley deal with the dual-career problem. Easily accessible from the Berkeley website is a document called the University of California Family Friendly Edge. It provides information pertinent to faculty at different career stages on policies and programs offered to assist them with work-life issues. One of the many services the program provides is a relocation counselor to help spouses and life partners in conducting a fruitful job search (University of California, 2003c).

Berkeley also participates in the Northern California Higher Education Resource Consortium, which presents job listings at academic institutions within close proximity. Los Angeles also provides dual-career partners with employment assistance in the form of a Higher Education Resource Consortium, which alerts to higher education positions in the Los Angeles area. In addition,

UCLA has a Faculty Diversity and Development department working "with departments to facilitate discussions about academic career partner hiring with other schools and divisions within UCLA" (University of California, 2008b). The campus human resources department also makes available services for spouses and life partners in nonacademic careers to help them find appropriate employment in the greater Los Angeles area.

Williams College

Williams College created a number of resources to assist partners of its faculty with employment assistance. As Professor Alonzo (pseudonym) notes, Williams is "rather isolated, [so] the two career couple and commuting issue is coming up." She points out that "[spousal/partner hiring] is an area we could do better in." Today, Williams has an Office of Spouse and Partner Employment Counseling, established in 2002, and it "provides career counseling and job search support to spouses and partners of current and prospective faculty and administrative staff" (Williams College, 2010c). The website highlights Williams' recognition that "for many prospective and current faculty and staff, issues relating to the professional integration of their spouses or partners is essential to their acceptance of employment and their continued investment in the College community" (Williams College, 2010c). The program does not guarantee a spouse or partner a position at Williams, Dr. Alonzo cautions. She emphasizes that "spousal hire is ad hoc. . . . If there is a spouse in another department there may be some effort to find teaching for the person, but we don't have mechanisms in place to encourage other departments to make tenure-track lines available to spouses." Williams provides a number of other resources, however. An Academic Career Network "offers spouses and partners of Williams College faculty and administrative staff Web-based access to faculty, research, and administrative openings at a cluster of nearby institutions, as well as the ability to post credentials in a searchable database accessible to prospective employers at member schools" (Williams College, 2010d). The College also provides a host of services for nonacademic spouses and partners. Again, it is important to note no promise of employment is made; however, the amount of attention Williams gives this issue illustrates the relatively life-friendly culture of the institution.

Boise State University

Policies at Boise State impressed us as the most creative means of dealing with the two-body problem. Boise State's faculty dual-career program is more extensive than many at other institutions. In the case of an academic spouse or partner, chairs of departments extending offers to primary hires contact the dean who will, in turn, get in touch with chairs of those departments that might provide employment to the spouse or partner. The appropriate department will then review the credentials of the spouse/ partner, and if the person fits its programmatic needs, he or she is recommended for appointment. The latter is vitally important, as emphasized by provost Andrews in a phone interview: "The department hiring the trailing spouse/partner has to want the person since these positions are seen as permanent hires. We do not force a person on a department because that could be very disruptive." If hired, a three-year commitment is made based on the assumption that after those three years, the person can move into the next available tenure line, or a new line will have been created. The system makes it possible, in other words, to hire a spouse or partner even if a tenure line is not available at that time. Another ingenious feature of the policy is the formula used to fund the spouse's/partner's salary for the first three years. It is evenly split three ways among the provost's office, the principal hire's department, and the spouse's/partner's department, all sharing the initial financial burden (Boise State University, 2005).

Policy Meets Faculty

Fleig-Palmer and others (2003) surveyed eighteen academic institutions about available dual-career services. They found that a broad array of services were offered, ranging from helping to complete a resume to providing information about job searching in the area. However, none of the institutions where our research was conducted provided substantive help to partners of academics they hired.

One wonders about early-career Professor Ampofo and his wife, a fellow Ph.D. An institution recruited him, and though he was happy there, he could not expect his wife to move to an area where the most she could hope for was a job as an administrative assistant. So he decided to leave and join another institution located within driving distance of other universities. His move must have been disappointing for him, and costly for the institution that lost its considerable investment in recruiting, hiring, and socializing a new faculty member. Dr. Ampofo points out that many of his colleagues find themselves in the same predicament and are waiting to find another position that would allow both partners to be appropriately employed.

Boise State is aware of the dual-career problem, and has designed an innovative policy to address it. As a faculty member there, Dr. Ampofo's partner would have received a position in the appropriate department, and the institution would have shared its costs three ways among departments and the provost's office. Most likely, a tremendous degree of institutional loyalty on the part of the Ampofos would have been one result. If their institution had been a member of an organization such as the Higher Education Recruiting Consortium, present at both Michigan and Berkeley, Professor Dennison and his partner could have found work at one university or at least at places that are less than a four-hour drive apart. The strain on their lives could have been lessened, productivity increased, and chances of continual employment improved if academic institutions recognized the dual-career problem and provided support structures to help alleviate it.

Though some might argue that the costs associated with these types of programs make them prohibitive, the cost both in real dollars and in the strain placed on the faculty suggests otherwise. Based on our data, it became clear that faculty were willing to compromise. Whether in terms of how they handled domestic obligations, or made decisions about where to live, the vast majority of interviewees recognized the need to make concessions. It appears that their compromises and sacrifices are little understood by their institutions, which may be well-served to explore new ways of dealing with dual-career couples. The creation of a Higher Education Recruiting Consortium requires only a time commitment, and is otherwise cost-neutral. As most academic institutions already have job placement services available for students, furthermore, it would not seem overly taxing to extend those services to partners of faculty and staff. Doing all or any of the above, an institution signals an understanding of the realities of their faculty's lives while mitigating their vulnerability and cementing their institutional commitment.

Recommendations

Due to the growing number of dual-career couples, institutions need to address the realities of their situations. To assist dual-career couples, we recommend that:

- Policies be created that allow nonacademic partners access to existing employment services that are already available on campus.

- Where possible, institutions partner with other institutions of higher education to create higher education recruitment consortiums.

- Innovative ways be found to create faculty positions for academic partners that do not force partners onto departments.

- Policies and programs be communicated that assist dual-career couples so that all stakeholders know and understand the reason for such policies.

- The human resources office be utilized so that partners and spouses can receive career counseling and coaching.

3

Parenting

As preceding chapters illustrate, the academic career path has grown more challenging over time for all faculty, regardless of gender and family constellation. Junior professors are expected to meet increased obligations that lack transparency and flexibility, which then contributes to faculty angst and makes it difficult to custom-tailor a career path fitting individual needs and circumstances. Single faculty members face barriers to crafting healthily balanced lives, finding spouses or partners, and starting families. Partnered faculty are confronted with institutional structures that refuse to accommodate the mounting number of dual-career couples and lack creativity in meeting the needs of academic couples. Yet another group of faculty that often finds it difficult to cope constitutes the topic of this chapter: faculty with children.

Given that both academe and the family are "greedy institutions" (Letherby, Marchbank, Ramsay, & Shiels, 2005, p. 211), women—and, more and more, men—continue to work "double shifts," their domestic labor vital yet largely unrecognized. How having children affects the careers of female faculty has only recently begun to attract attention, and how it increasingly affects men remains understudied. This chapter discusses parenting among both female and male academics with particular emphasis on how the issue has changed over the course of recent generations.

Although many women in higher education have long struggled to combine the pursuit of an academic career with parenthood, it was not until 2003 that an article in the *Chronicle of*

Higher Education reported results of what is believed to be the first study based on national data showing what women in academic life have known for a long time: having children can have a devastating impact on the careers of academic women (Wilson, 2003). The "Do Babies Matter?" project examined the effects of family formation on career progression, the effects of having a faculty career on family patterns, and the nature of work-family conflict for academic parents. According to the research, marriage and young children have a strong negative effect on women entering tenure-track positions, and tenure-track women are less likely to gain tenure than their male counterparts (regardless of family formation). Once on the tenure track, women and men possess different family formation patterns. For example, tenure-track women are less likely than tenure-track men to have children. When attempting to answer why women opt out of the academy or are pushed out, and why men and women have different family formation patterns, the researchers find one explanation in the tension between work and family responsibilities. This tension, they underscore, is more strongly felt by women than men (Mason, Goulden, & Wolfinger, 2006, pp. 11–17).

The women's study informing this book (Philipsen, 2008) provides powerful testimony to the challenges faced by those female faculty who have children and an academic career, too. They report how difficult it is to find the "right" time to get pregnant and have babies, given that their biological clocks tend to coincide with their tenure clocks. Some forfeit having children altogether, and those who do have children struggle with managing both the expectations of a demanding career and the demands of motherhood. At their institutions, child leave policies are either not transparent or readily available, or both; rather than being clearly communicated and uniformly applied, they need to be negotiated on an individual basis. The institutions included in our studies, furthermore, did not grant paid child leave. Therefore, women had to use accrued sick leave to cobble together whatever leave they could afford. In Associate Professor McMillan's case, her sick leave was not enough to cover an entire semester; she had to take half-time leave for 16 weeks and found herself back in the class-room shortly after her baby was born by C-section. "There were no policies. There were no guidelines," she remembers, and what happens when there are no guidelines is that faculty have to "sort of tentatively feel out what is possible. It is sort of like pushing until people say 'no.' Yet you never know where 'no' is." The pro-cess, in short, is arbitrary.

Another mechanism designed to help women who are having or adopting children is stopping the tenure clock, an increasingly common but problematic practice (Jaschick, 2009). Faculty fear that it backfires when tenure and promotion committees ratchet up their standards, assuming that a woman enjoyed an "extra year" and can thus be expected to have produced more scholar-ship. Women also struggle with lack of quality child care, bouts of guilt, the feeling that their attention is always divided, and that no matter how much they work at home and in academe, what they put out is neither enough nor satisfactorily executed. As Assistant Professor Dr. Moller, mother of a three-year-old and pregnant with her second child, says: "I guess for me the way I balance, if you can call it that, is I put out the biggest most imme-diate fires as they come and juggle as necessary. There is always something falling through the crack."

It became obvious that in their attempts to "do it all," what tended to be sacrificed was care of self: hobbies, exercise, relation-ships, and pleasure. Not surprisingly, we found that single parents confronted particularly vexing dilemmas, and the stress of being a parent and a faculty member did not necessarily get resolved after tenure. Child care remains an ongoing problem, especially lack-ing care for infants or mildly sick children. Associate Professor McMillan describes how she was administratively reprimanded for bringing a mildly sick child to class in order to administer an exam. This is what she has to say:

> I'm still catching grief about this. I have had adminis-
> trators call me and tell me that it was inappropriate to
> have my child on campus, and that it was a huge distrac-
> tion for the students, and they had gotten all these com-
> plaints. So I said to one of the administrators . . . who
> called me on the carpet for this, I'm a working mother.
> The reality of my life is, I'm a working parent. The other
> working parent was in a meeting full of deans and could
> not take this child. The child caregiver was otherwise
> committed. I had the choice of canceling the exam for
> 300 students, bringing her into the classroom, or I could
> have brought her to your office, and you could have
> taken care of her. I was a little pissed off at that point.

Dr. Schumacher faults a patriarchal model according to which "home is where the children are, work is not where the children are." Children are labeled a "private problem" and if "you wanted to be a working mom, it is your problem. Resolve it."

Doubtlessly, problems such as Dr. McMillan's used to be primarily working mothers' problems and even today, being a parent
affects women differently from men. Recent research of faculty
members at the University of California reveals that mothers
work ninety-five hours on average and spend 43 percent of this
time on child care and housework compared to fathers who work
an average of eighty hours per week, spending 31 percent of this
time on domestic labor. Even among doctoral students, the numbers have not fully equalized (Mason, 2009). Nevertheless, if analyzed over time, our research indicates significant generational
changes have occurred and are transforming the parenting land-
scape in academe. Little data is available to shed light on these
changes because generations ago hardly anybody *asked* how much

time men spent on domestic labor. We asked men at the late-career stages in the professoriate, however, and compared their testimony with that of men at earlier career stages, and it became clear that, increasingly, not only are academic women affected by the tension between parenting and professing, but so are academic men. Though many members of older generations of male faculty may have been largely unencumbered by parenting and free to pursue their professional obligations without much interference, more and more younger male faculty would agree with Professor Ampofo who says: "Our priority is our kids, and we do everything that we can to provide for them, but we also need to help our careers, too."

Just as men of younger generations are facing changing roles and divisions of labor at home, and increasingly participating in domestic work, they are much more involved as parents than previous generations of men were. This chapter illustrates the changes that occurred over time, and, considering also the findings on parenting derived from the women's study, makes the case that both men and women desperately need better policies and programs that allow them to fulfill both their professional and their parenting roles well. We will once again describe what exists at the seven institutions employing the faculty interviewed in our studies and then compare those realities with what exemplary institutions offer. The chapter concludes with recommendations.

It has been argued that although "[h]istorically, fathers have been a rather invisible group in the study of child development and family processes, with their influence rarely considered and their voices scarcely heard . . . the past two decades have seen a significant growth in the public, political, and academic attention directed at fathers, addressing their roles in families, their rights and responsibilities, and their influence on their children" (Coley, 2001, p. 743). Reporting the fathers' point of view, Kramer cites research on involved fathers most of whom felt that "being a father was more influential than any other facet of their lives had been" (Kramer, 2005, p. 63, referencing Palkovitz, Copes, & Woolfolk, 2001). The significant generational changes of men's views on fatherhood became obvious in our research.

Both early and midcareer male faculty see family and personal relationships as centrally important, although many came to this understanding only after encountering immense personal difficulties. The lives of late-career men, in general, revolved around work.

Being an engaged father was heavily emphasized by junior faculty who continually demonstrate their commitment to their children. Professor Johnson says he takes this role very seriously, and gets "a lot from kids and family, and that's important to me personally. I'm proud to be a father; I'm proud of the responsibility." Many engage in what has been called "split-shift parenting" (Gornick & Meyers, 2005, p. 371), meaning parents taking turns caring for their children. Professor Allison, for instance, often finds it necessary to bring his four-year-old to the office because "sometimes school schedules don't match . . . work schedules. It is something you have to worry about when you have kids. You have to figure out what to do with them." Fatherhood, to him, is no part-time job.

The contradiction of academe creating a more conducive environment for engaged fatherhood than other industries while simultaneously creating unique pressures of its own is a recurring theme voiced by early-career faculty. Professor Trenton sees having a child as an academic as "one of the best things . . . [because] nobody is holding a gun to your head to be in a particular place except for a few hours a week." It should be remembered, however, that this flexibility is tightly coupled with increasing productivity expectations, and men are beginning to sound like their female colleagues when they talk about trying to juggle work and parenthood. The following two quotes illustrate this struggle, first captured by female Professor Young-Powell, then male Professor Allison:

Dr. Young-Powell:

> For me it's tiring. I do find myself a lot of times at 11,
> 12, 1 o'clock in the morning doing more planning and
> other administrative duties. I don't want to stay [at work]
> until six every night because I want to go home to be
> mommy. . . . Sometimes when [I have] time off, when
> they're napping, instead of doing things that I need
> to be doing at home, I'm spending time doing things for
> [work] at home. . . . I spend a lot of time [working] when
> I'd really rather be sleeping when they're in bed.

Dr. Allison:

> When I say work at home it's usually once the kids have
> gone to school or daycare. Once you've gotten them out
> of the house because once they're in the house, you're
> prevented from turning the page, or you might find some
> time after they've gone to bed that you might need to
> work on some stuff. . . . It happens that half the time, or
> more than half the time, I fall asleep when they do, so
> I just get up early. That is usually the best time because
> nobody is awake.

The previous statements are qualitatively different from that
of late-career Professor Jackson, who proudly describes himself as
being ". . . spoiled by the situation I had myself, which was lots
and lots of hours to do my work without anyone bothering me."

Generational shifting became obvious in the testimony of midcareer male faculty. Some men continue to view those domestic
crises that involve their children as their wives' responsibilities.
Their positions seem well justified to them, especially if they are
the sole wage earners. Others disagree in both philosophy and
practice, perhaps in part because many of them have gone through

divorces and have consequently vowed not to repeat in their second marriages mistakes they had previously made. Professor Ashcroft, for instance, is more involved in his children's lives now than he used to be and reports more interactions with his younger two children than with his older two. He has learned to think differently about his career: "You have to get to where you know, hey, if you drop dead, it goes on. They will have the conference."

Having children has caused some male faculty to reassess what they view as centrally important. Professor McDaniels's marriage and children, for instance, changed his priorities:

> After I got married, things had to shift a little bit. You know, priorities change and you can't stay in an office until 10, 11 o'clock at night because your wife wants you home for dinner. When you start having children priorities shift again. So I guess that's where I am in my life now. . . . I think that family is really important, especially in this day and time when you have children, it's absolutely important for fathers to take the lead to really engage in the lives of their children.

This sentiment is echoed by Professor Zavella, who acknowledges not being as advanced in his career as others might like him to be, but views his family as his first priority. When asked by his dean why he is not maximizing his potential, he responds, "Well, I think I am. It's just that what you see as your personal goals, you've tried to project those on me, and it doesn't apply. To me, I think having a happy family, well-balanced children . . . is a whole lot more important." He never allowed his career to overshadow his family responsibilities, and only now that his children are grown is he willing to do what is necessary to be promoted to full professor. Professor Molina agrees; having children "has helped me just get so much more perspective about how I want to live this life."

Even those midcareer faculty who invested heavily in their careers tried to be active in their children's lives. Professor Sneed realizes that he "was able to do a lot with [his children] because mostly I teach at night. So, field trips, swimming, band, whatever, tennis, pretty much I could be there for them, and after I decided that's what I wanted to do, I think I was really good at that." Similarly, Professor Dotolo recounts how he and his spouse read child-care books together, an indication of his determination to take an equal role in raising his children. "I was right there from the start because [otherwise] I wouldn't have known how to quiet him down; I wouldn't have known how to feed him," he says.

Being actively engaged in raising their children has made the men more aware of issues faced by working parents. Dr. Eggleston remembers how a meeting that was supposed to end at 4:30 P.M. ran over. The dean and other faculty continued to talk without any recognition that their actions were inconveniencing parents like him. He "felt that there was an insensitivity to being inefficient with the time, and [my wife and I] also felt like nobody is going to want to hear it if we complain that we've got kids to take care of."

Professor Sneed remembers what he calls "a ridiculous choice." His child's surgery was scheduled for the same time as a meeting, and he was told by his chair that "if I missed [the meeting] she was going to fire me or write me up." He ultimately suffered no professional consequences for choosing not to attend the meeting, but the incident drastically altered his perceptions of both his career and his institution. Though not true of all participants at the late-career stage, many believe that having children as an academic creates a unique set of problems; for them, actively parenting is incompatible with active professional involvement. Says Dr. Riley: "It would be very hard for us to be two academics, one or both of whom doing some administrative thing, and still have children at home." Professor Jackson is convinced that "you will have to sacrifice some part of your career if you think that children are important enough to be made into responsible, caring citizens and parents themselves." Professor Ingrahm paints a picture considerably more bleak: "You get a job, and then you have this terrific duty of burning yourself out in order to get tenure, and so that walls you off from your family to some extent . . . and so there go seven years, and then now you're a stranger to your kids . . . so, you never really know them at all, which I think is probably something of a tragedy."

Their pessimistic outlook is based on experience. Late-career Professor Green remembers times when academe was not at all attuned to the family part of an academic's life. Child care, for instance, "would have made so much difference. . . . Kids came home from school. We weren't there sometimes, and to be able to have childcare on campus would have been wonderful."

A rigid division of labor seemed necessary; professor Thompson illustrates: "[My wife] has taken on a tremendous amount of responsibility in terms of raising the kids, making sure that they get what they want. . . . She took care of all that because I wasn't around."

As always, there are exceptions, and some late-career men assumed a relatively active role in the upbringing of their children, such as Professor Richardson, who ponders whether he was an oddity for his generation: "I was not perhaps as typical of a male in America at that time. I was involved with raising my children," he says. Dr. Jellig also swam against the stream and recounts: "I was the only dad who was in the carpools."

In sum, significant changes have occurred across generations in how male faculty think about and act not only in regard to their relationships, marriages, and the division of labor with their spouses and partners, as the previous chapters described, but also their involvement with child rearing. Though this study is not designed to be generalizable, and differences certainly exist within groups, it is clear that younger faculty are much more involved in domestic duties than their older colleagues and are more inclined to craft relatively egalitarian relationships with their life partners.

They tend to share responsibilities for their children and are actively engaged in coparenting. They have, in other words, made their families much more of a priority vis-à-vis their employment than their older colleagues did.

We puzzled over why these generational changes occurred. In regard to parenting, Rosanna Hertz' research showed that dual-earner couples who are embracing a "new parenting approach" (meaning both parents are fully participating in raising their children) are only able to do so when certain conditions are in place, such as flexible work hours. Not all families have the means or the opportunity to enact their beliefs about how children should be raised, she argues, and "[p]ositioning in the external labor market and, more specifically, within a particular organization's internal labor market strongly influences whether individual women and men implement . . . their ideologies about parenting" (Hertz, 2004, p. 256). A growing number of early- and midcareer faculty members and their significant others seem to have decided to do something most members of previous generations did not or felt they could not do. They make use of the relative security that their professional status affords them and of whatever degree of flexibility they find in their work, and they venture out to craft new relationships and family dynamics, despite significant challenges. Although these faculty members embrace their new roles and prefer them over the truncated ones played by previous generations, they find that increased involvement in domestic affairs and parenting is not easy. Dr. Trenton appreciates the increased acceptance of male faculty who decide to spend more time with their families; however, if one needs child care, for example, and the wife's salary is low, the dual earner existence breeds financial problems. In addition, on a day-to-day basis "it's a big coordination problem." Such testimony is understandable given the lack of support provided by the seven institutions employing the participants in our studies.

Neither Public Comprehensive nor Metropolitan University impressed us with their provisions for child care and child leave.

Comprehensive has a child-care center on campus; however, at the time of this research, it was full. Faculty are given priority for placing their children in the center but do neither receive a rate reduction nor any other special financial considerations. The center has no part-time option; therefore, faculty pay full-time rates whether they utilize the facility all week or not. In addition, the center does not admit children younger than sixteen months of age.

Metropolitan has two on-campus child-care centers, yet the waiting lists are long. The minimum age for admission is eighteen months. There are no partnerships between Metropolitan and any day-care facilities; however, it does provide links to additional providers from its website. Recently, and after the conclusion of our research, Metropolitan has added a sick-child-care program to its offerings, but whereas exemplary institutions typically charge $5.00 for registration, Metropolitan has a $40.00 registration fee.

In light of the fact that maternity/paternity leave policies at either institution do not allow a parent to be home for sixteen or eighteen months, it seems that new parents are expected to shoulder the responsibility for finding appropriate care for their children before that age without any resources available through the academic institutions.

Both Public Comprehensive and Metropolitan utilize the Family and Medical Leave Act (FMLA) to guide their maternity leave policies. Thus, a faculty member, father or mother, can take up to twelve weeks of unpaid leave in order to care for a newborn or adopted child. Any accrued sick leave will be paid. However, most of the faculty do not accrue sick leave, so there is a possibility that any time off is unpaid unless the faculty member has enrolled in the short-term disability program offered by the institution. Furthermore, a twelve-week leave policy does not cover an entire semester. Therefore, most female faculty need to negotiate a reduced course load for the semester and are thus forced to teach at least some despite recent childbirth and a new baby. It should also be stressed that no formal policy is in place; so parents are at the mercy of their deans and department chairs.

Flagship University's policies are very similar to those at Public Comprehensive. An on-campus day-care center exists, but it is currently full. A visit to the institution's website reveals that faculty are encouraged to "research your desired childcare provider and then to place your name on the appropriate waiting list(s) as close to the *time of conception* as possible." Faculty do receive priority when it comes to enrollment of their children, however, and the center has no age restriction, thus providing infant care.

Maternity/paternity leave policies at Flagship are based on FMLA, allowing parents twelve weeks of unpaid leave. Again, all of the problems inherent in a twelve-week leave are present, and there was no codified policy about a reduced course load available. Individual faculty members do, however, negotiate to use a semester of "research leave" after childbirth.

Private Comprehensive University has no child care available on campus, an issue that, according to faculty senate minutes, has been discussed on numerous occasions. The institution's administration, however, responded that a day-care facility on campus was not economically feasible, a curious argument given the college's $1.65 billion endowment. The maternity/paternity leave policy is based on FMLA, and though short-term disability insurance is available, according to the policy "faculty may only use short-term disability for the time that she is under a doctor's care." Thus, it is intended only for women who are having difficult pregnancies or difficult births rather than for those who wish to stay home and tend to the newborn during the first few months. Again, the faculty senate meeting minutes indicate that the faculty has requested maternity/paternity leave policies, but the administration responded it followed FMLA and may in the future consider other leave options.

In the case of both HBCU and Community College, the policy search once again proved depressing. No child-care provisions are made by either institution; there was no maternity/paternity leave information to be found. However, because these institutions are required to follow FMLA, it can be assumed that twelve weeks of unpaid leave is at least available to the faculty.

In summary, those colleges and universities where the study was conducted provide, at best, limited policies designed to enable faculty to successfully navigate work-life challenges associated with parenting, and the situation is just as dire for staff and students. Juxtaposing what is and what could be, the next section portrays child-care and child-leave policies and programs available at exemplary institutions.

Exemplary Institutions: Child Care

University of Washington

According to Dr. Kate Quinn, the project director at Balance@ UW, child care poses a continuous challenge given that the need far exceeds what the university can offer. Not just faculty and staff are in need of child care but also postdocs, graduate, and undergraduate students. However, UW has been creative in its approach to maximize the child care available to the UW community. It has worked with the state to obtain funding, applied for and received small grants to give to community-based child care which then, in turn, provides priority access to UW employees, and, in addition, found various ways to connect to different providers in the community. The latter strategies are important because, as the informant emphasized, not all parents want to obtain on-campus child care.

Quinn and Shapiro (2009) report that in 2006 the provost formed a campuswide Child Care Advisory Committee which identified areas in need of attention. The authors point out that the importance of child care is well understood by many of the university's leaders, and this buy-in is essential.

At the University of Washington's Seattle campus, four fully accredited child-care centers serve infants, toddlers, and preschoolers.

Two of them primarily assist faculty and staff, the other two are for students. All are open year-round, and part-time options are available. The centers' philosophies are based on Maria Montessori's principles for early childhood education, and child-teacher ratios are excellent (infants: one adult per three children; toddlers: one adult per five children; preschool: one adult per ten children). Tuition rates vary by center and child's age from $700 to $1,430 per month for full-time enrollment.

In addition to on-campus child care, UW provides information on community-based child care by partnering with the local nonprofit Child Care Resources (CCR) to provide free child care referral services. The service maintains listings of licensed providers and child care centers; it also does advocacy work with government, business, and other nonprofits for the importance of early-childhood education. Included are listings of those who provide after-school and summer care for school-age children, as well as care for children with special needs.

Furthermore, a caregiver directory is provided for those who only occasionally need babysitting or child care services. In addition, the Nanny Share Network, whose coordination runs through the university's Benefits & Work/Life office, assists those who wish to hire and share nannies. Recommendations are made as to how to find and interview a nanny and how to craft a contract. Yet another feature of the university's child-care provisions exists in the provision of care to mildly sick children in the Tender Loving Care at Virginia Mason Medical Center for a one-time registration fee of $5.00.

As mentioned before, the UW system does not merely serve its faculty but also staff and students. A child-care assistance program for students exists, for example, funded through student services and activities fees. Students are eligible for support depending on income and the number of credits for which they are registered. Under this system, full-time students can receive up to 60 percent of child-care tuition and, according to Quinn and Shapiro (2009), they can apply the funds at any licensed child-care center. Part-time student assistance is prorated depending upon the student's number of credits.

The University of Washington also provides monthly parent education and parent assistance, including programs to help the expecting parent plan leave and choose child care. Parents receive information about flexible work arrangements and the university's employee assistance program. UW provides a database with information for parents of teenagers as well as various programs and services for children of all ages. Examples are "child-friendly" locations in case a child comes to campus such as museums, art galleries, the intramural activities building, sports events, to name a few. There are changing stations, lactation stations, and a pediatric health center.

The University of Washington is able to afford its elaborate support system of parents due to the use of various strategies. One of them, according to Quinn & Shapiro (2009), was the collaboration with community-based child care centers that allow UW parents priority access. Another lies in obtaining grant funding for various projects such as the federal Department of Education's *Child Care Access Means Parents in Schools* (CCAMPIS) grant that secured half a million dollars between 2001 and 2005 for student financial assistance. The authors thus suggest to those who wish to replicate the UW success that they (a) develop their grant seeking behavior; and (b) enhance collaboration and partnerships, not only with community resources but also within the university by, for instance, tapping into research dollars or accessing intern sites for students in academic programs with a practicum component related to early childhood issues (Quinn & Shapiro, 2009).

University of Michigan

The main campus of the University of Michigan at Ann Arbor operates three day-care facilities. Though each individual center runs under its own goals and philosophies, the centers together provide child care at reasonable rates, allowing for both full-time and part-time care. In addition, among them, children from as young as three months all the way through kindergarten are accommodated. Laurita Thomas, associate vice president and chief human resource officer, notes that "[t]he Center for the Education of Women on campus has been a big help to faculty women and now to all faculty." The Center spearheads initiatives pertinent to work-life balance issues such as on-campus infant care. According to Dr. Thomas, "We didn't have any infant care on campus. . . . The President's Advisory group [picking up on this initiative] caused a child care initiative that significantly increased the environmental resources . . . [and led to] providing infant care" on campus. According to the child-care website, openings are available, and faculty members looking for high-quality day-care facilities can place their children in the state-of-the-art centers with high-quality providers and low child-teacher ratios. As the website states:

> Center staff include teachers and associate teachers, many with degrees in Early Childhood Education and/or Child Development. The retention of the professional staff is exceedingly high and many staff members have been with the program over 5 years. The teaching staff is complemented by undergraduate psychology practicum students, temporary student employees, student teachers, or graduate-level researchers.
>
> Each group of children is supervised by a staff of professionally trained teachers including a teacher, an associate teacher, and University students. The adult/child ratio ranges between 1:3 and 1:7 (depending on the ages of the children) for each of the classrooms. (University of Michigan, n.d.-a)

Biographies of those who work at the center along with their qualifications are available to current and potential clients. In addition to their on-campus centers, Michigan offers employees a Child Care Referral Specialist who will assist in helping faculty find a program that works for their schedule and needs. The website lets the faculty know that in-person and phone consultations are available. Finally, in case parents prefer to search out potential day-care centers on their own, the Child Care Services website provides a Web-based referral service.

Perhaps the most innovative assistance the institution possesses is something called Kids Kare at Home, which facilitates emergency back-up child care, something Dr. Sullivan called "extremely useful." It requires that parents register with the service through the Work/Life Resource Specialist. Registration is free, and parents only pay when they use the service. Work/Life Resource Director Jennie McAlpine said that "between 1,200 and 1,800 people register for it each year, [and] the people who use it give it rave reviews." Here is how it works: a trained caregiver comes to the home if children are sick, or if the regular child-care provider is not available. Considering that one of the biggest stressors for dual-career parents is a sick child, this service is invaluable. Instead of facing the dilemma of either leaving a sick child at home or taking her to work, both inappropriate solutions, parents are able to leave children in the care of a trained professional. Other than the personnel costs involved in setting it up, this service does not involve any costs for the university because the parents pay. According to McAlpine, UM does subsidize the program, and the fee for services "is on a sliding scale, so it is an affordable program." However, without the subsidy, the program is "cost-neutral."

Here again, the University of Michigan signals to its faculty an understanding of the life issues that arise by providing a much-needed resource. The institution encourages people to disseminate information about Kids Kare, through printable flyers, available on the program's website (University of Michigan, n.d.-b).

University of California

The issue of finding quality child care, as noted by the male and female faculty, is addressed by the University of California system by offering on-campus child care. The Los Angeles campus and the Berkeley campus run two child-care centers each, serving children as young as two months. They also instituted a number of summer programs. Both have a large facility operated by the University, and both have smaller centers for infants which are run by the Department of Psychology. However, waiting lists exist at both campuses. Dr. Miller, a longtime faculty member at UCLA, called child care "a huge issue" because many faculty members believe that the campus should provide child care for all faculty, staff, and students. He notes, however, that "the question was, how should this be paid for," and fears that "now with the budget crisis the issue is off the table." Echoing this concern about the dearth of spaces available at Berkeley, Dr. Mason, law professor and codirector of the Center for Economic and Family Security, feels that "child care is always a problem. It's limited, and not that cheap—we subsidize the graduate students, but faculty do not get subsidies, and there is a long waiting list." Just like Dr. Miller, Dr. Mason views child care as "one of the major issues."

One might question why the UC system is considered exemplary given that it struggles with the same shortage in openings expressed by many interviewed for this study and the study on female faculty. What is unique, and exemplary, is that both campuses provide assistance and guidance in securing child care if no spaces are available at the on-campus centers. UCLA offers a Child Care Resource program; its website is worth quoting at length:

> The Child Care Resource Program provides child development information and off-campus resources to UCLA families. The program coordinator is in contact with Westside child care providers and a small number

of caregivers who will come to your home. For other parts of metropolitan Los Angeles, resources are available from state-funded Resource and Referral agencies. The Child Care Resource Program is a personalized service for UCLA families. The coordinator will describe the range of resources available, how to evaluate a particular program or provider and suggest what questions will provide parents with the information they need to make a stable arrangement.

The coordinator will provide a list of resources. Although changes can occur in a relatively short period of time, a general picture is given of what to expect from a particular provider and program. The Child Care Resource Program believes that parents must make their own decisions based on what feels most comfortable to them and what arrangements best meet their family's needs. We do not make referrals or recommendations. (University of California, 2008a)

The Berkeley campus provides a similar resource; a twenty-three-page guide on "Finding Child Care" is easily accessible and printable. Covered are issues such as selecting the best child care, sick-child care, evaluating child-care programs, child-care referral agencies and services, and a child-care evaluation checklist (University of California, 2002). Berkeley, like the University of Michigan, provides access to a program for employees with sick children. The Sick Child Care Program called "Wheezles and Sneezles" makes available a Get Well Center located on campus, or it will "dispatch trained care providers to your home for 8-hour shifts" (University of California, 2002). These services are offered on a sliding scale fee of $0–5/hr for the center and $0–7/hr for in-home care. Thus, although the child-care "shortage" is still an issue for faculty, the institution takes a proactive stance to assist faculty with what can potentially be a very worrisome process for parents.

Williams College

Williams has an on-campus day care center that provides care for all ages from infants to preschoolers. Though the Williams College Children's Center does not exclusively serve employees, they do receive preferential treatment. In addition, though the center gives preference to children who need care full-time, part-time care is offered (Williams College, 2010f). The center also provides after school care for children ages five to twelve. Due to the center's flexibility, it seems, most faculty are served, regardless of their scheduling needs. Realizing that child care may still be an issue, Williams has created a Babysitting Coordinator who coordinates a "network of students available to babysit for faculty and staff" (Williams College, 2010e). The site makes clear that the babysitters are not employees of the institution, but does provide helpful tips for faculty interested in using them, such as what to look for in a potential sitter. Though this program is not as comprehensive as some at the larger institutions, it does provide faculty help with an issue that has been seen to cause an immense amount of stress for parents. Although parents are required to give twenty-four hours notice to the coordinator, at least a service is available if faculty need to leave their children home from school due to an illness or another cause.

Boise State University

Boise State University has for many years offered both full- and part-time care on-campus to students, faculty, and staff, serving about two hundred children from birth to five years of age in classrooms with relatively small teacher-student ratios. The fees range between $30 and $43 per day depending upon status and income. Students generally pay less than faculty who, in turn, pay less than community members and adjunct faculty. Availability varies; as of the time of the writing of this book, the wait time for full-time faculty who wished to enroll infants was two semesters while openings did exist for older children.

Boise State's nationally accredited "Children's Center" is proud to be "more" than simply a child-care center, given its preschool component designed to provide a developmentally appropriate learning environment. It utilizes a "creative curriculum" based on ideas derived from leading scholars in the field. University students from a wide variety of programs perform their internships and volunteer work at the center or use it to fulfill class requirements. In addition, a link off the center's website provides information about criteria to use when looking for child care elsewhere such as relationships, curriculum, teaching and teachers, assessment, health, and so on (Boise State University, n.d.-a).

Valley College

Child care is available on the Valley College campus. The Child Development Center is operated by the Social Science and Human Development department, providing care to children of faculty, students, and staff from birth to age five. According to the website, they "strive to provide the highest quality of early care and education for San Bernardino Valley College students and the children of our community. The program exists and operates with four primary elements: Services to children and families, demonstration, professional development and parent education" (San Bernardino Valley College, n.d.). According to faculty member Dr. Jiminez (pseudonym), "it was funded through grants. You have to apply for it, and there are requirements for getting in. [One of the requirements is] that you have to be associated with the college."

Exemplary Institutions: Child Leave

University of Washington

Parental leave policies at the University of Washington go beyond the provisions we found at any of the institutions where the faculty for this study were interviewed. A female faculty member at UW who gives birth is covered under the sick leave policy and thus eligible for ninety days of paid leave. Her salary continues during that time period during which she is usually on the payroll; nine-month faculty (those who do not work during the summer, in other words) do not get paid during the summer if that is when they give birth. The woman must provide written certification from a health care provider, attesting to the fact that she is unable to work because of her pregnancy, childbirth, or recovery. The care of an ill child may be covered by paid leave but adoption of a child is not, and fathers cannot use it to provide care for an infant.

Under the Family and Medical Leave Act (FMLA), a faculty member can take twelve weeks of unpaid leave for the care of a newborn, adopted or foster child, spouse, son, daughter, domestic partner, or parent who has a serious health condition. Eligible faculty are entitled to the position they had before the leave or to one that is virtually identical in terms of job title, work location, salary, hours, and so forth.

In addition, faculty can take full or partial leave without salary for up to six months, renewable and extendable to a maximum of two years (combined with parental leave). Faculty also have the option of taking family care leave, which entails using paid sick or medical leave to care for a sick child under eighteen years of age (over eighteen years of age in case of a mental or physical disability) or spouse, parent, parent-in-law, or grandparent.

University of Michigan

Understanding that the birth or adoption of a child is a major life event, Michigan has some of the most forward-thinking policies available. New child leave at Michigan provides the new parent with one semester off. If both parents work for the university, each parent receives a semester of child-care leave. According to Dr. Frumkin, Assistant Provost and Senior Director of Academic Human Resources, "the modified duties program was put into place to allow women who were pregnant to be relieved of all teaching duties in the semester prior to the semester when their birth was anticipated." Provost Sullivan finds that most couples at Michigan take separate semesters off so that children with parents who both work at the university have a parent at home for one year. She admits that "there are older faculty who discourage younger faculty from taking it." The university tries to counter these negative influences administratively, but Dr. Sullivan is unsure whether these attempts are always successful. And yet, given the problems noted by faculty in the women's study who have given birth or adopted, and the problems noted by faculty interviewed in the men's study, Michigan's policy provides considerable support for families and enables them to adjust to this major life event.

In addition to taking leave, faculty have the opportunity to modify teaching assignments and have a reduced load for two semesters rather than taking one full semester off. This flexibility provides faculty with a number of options so that they can create the schedule that is most workable for them and their families. Information made available to new or expecting parents reads:

> If you give birth or become a parent of a newly born or adopted child, you may be entitled to a period of time during which your teaching duties will be modified to allow you to adjust to this new set of life demands—*with no reduction in salary*. (emphasis added) (University of Michigan, 2005a)

Again, this policy makes clear that the institution understands that having a child creates a "new set of life demands." Michigan also realizes that most faculty cannot afford to take leaves if they entail reduced salaries. Thus, they provide time for their faculty to adjust to this momentous life event without a loss of income.

Kelly Ward and Lisa Wolf-Wendel in "Fear Factor: How Safe Is It to Make Time for Family," argue for "an 'integrative model' in which employers adopt a series of policies that can be used alone or in combination with one another as needed by employees. Such a model recognizes the way people work and supports the coherence faculty want for their work and home lives" (2004, p. 10). The University of Michigan's leave policies fit this bill.

In addition to its impressive flexibility, UM's approach toward child leave stands out in how easily the information can be found. Beginning with Michigan's Family Friendly home page, information about childbirth, adoption, and the policies surrounding these events is one click away.

This institution's policies for child leave not only go above and beyond any of the institutions covered by our interview study, they go above and beyond many of the other exemplary institutions we researched. In fact, we would argue that their policy on child leave could be a model for other institutions in the country.

University of California

The maternity/paternity leave policies offered by the UC system provide time for both parents to learn to accommodate a child into their lives. For the birth mother, "[l]eave for childbirth and recovery normally will be for at least six weeks" (University of California, n.d.). In addition, faculty may take advantage of an available short-term disability policy in order for a total amount of leave of four months. In addition, the UC system has created a program for new parents called Active Service Modified Duties. This policy allows faculty to modify their teaching responsibilities and is "granted on request to any appointee who has substantial responsibility for the care of his or her newborn child or child under age five placed for adoption or foster care." This policy allows for "a partial or full relief from teaching," and it stipulates that if it is used with a "semester of childbearing leave, there must be full relief from scheduled teaching duties" (University of California, n.d.). What this actually translates to, according to Professor Mason, UC Berkeley law professor and codirector of the Center for Economic and Family Security, is "two semesters off for new mothers and one semester for dads." Therefore, new mothers are provided time during their children's first year to grow accustomed to having a new baby. It also indicates an understanding of the importance of fathers by providing them with a semester to bond and be actively engaged in their children's care. The Berkeley campus also wants to ensure that graduate students, who may be considering joining the professoriate, understand that Berkeley is family-friendly. In order to keep its competitive edge and attract top graduate students, Dr. Mason notes that "we [Berkeley] do more for our graduate students; we have a six week paid maternity leave for all students with any type of graduate assistantship." She expressed hope that helping graduate students with work-life issues will help stem "the great drop of interest in faculty careers among graduate students."

Williams College

Williams possesses quite progressive parental leave policies. Faculty member Dr. Alonzo (pseudonym) shared that "there is the federally mandated maternity leave, which is only available for women who are biologically pregnant, and in addition to that, there is parental leave for anyone having or adopting a child. Pregnant women can combine the two leaves." Faculty "have the option of being released from all or part of their teaching duties in the semester during or following the birth of a child. . . . The faculty member may elect either a one-semester maternity leave at 3/4 pay or the equivalent of a one-course reduction without loss of pay for the semester following childbirth. The faculty member will normally elect to combine this maternity leave with a paid parental leave, for a total of one semester's leave at full pay" (Williams College, 2009). As a result, any new parent can receive a one-course teaching load reduction for a semester, which is in essence a 50 percent reduction in teaching responsibilities because faculty at Williams have a 2/2 load. Inherent in the policy is the acknowledgment that new fathers need time to adjust to their role, just as new mothers do.

Of course, the efficacy of any policy depends upon its use. Dr. Alonzo, noting the anecdotal nature of her statement, believes that "the first 2 or 3 years, no men took it, and they worried that people would look down on them. . . . Now that it has been in place for 8–9 years . . . men are starting to take it. I don't know whether they all take it, but it has increased." Her observation is in line with findings based on our interviews with male faculty, namely, that younger generations of faculty desire time to be fully included in raising their children. In addition, Williams also provides faculty with the option of requesting a "second course off without pay to achieve one semester's leave" (Williams College, 2009). So, new parents, not just the biological mother, have the opportunity to take a semester off with 3/4 pay.

Boise State University

Leave resulting from pregnancy, childbirth, or adoption of a child is covered by one of the less progressive policies at Boise State given that it provides little more than the Family and Medical Leave Act. However, as emphasized by Provost Andrews, Boise State's career flexibility policies, especially its flexible workload program, "provide somewhat of a safety net for the lack of generosity on the maternity policy side." Specifically, the flexible workload (also known as differentiated load) policy allows tenured and tenure-track faculty flexibility in how they allocate their time in regard to research, teaching, and service. They are able to shift, for example, all teaching requirements to one semester so that they are free to pursue their research or special opportunities that may arise during the next semester. It also means that during the semester when the faculty member does not teach, he or she does not physically have to be on campus and is therefore free to engage in special care duties for a child, family member, aging parent, and so forth, including the care of someone who lives out of town, as long as these responsibilities do not interfere with the agreed-on work expectations. This is a key idea for less wealthy institutions that might not otherwise have the resources to implement some of the other policies.

This flexible workload policy originated in the provost's office, and was then discussed and finally endorsed by other stakeholders, including the faculty senate. "I would never consider instituting any policy like that without the faculty senate's endorsement," Dr. Andrews said, pointing out that some policy changes cannot be done quickly because it takes time to secure all parties' buy-in; but "that is needed if you want it to work."

Valley College

One of the unique benefits for faculty at Valley College is that the bargaining agreement under which they operate provides ten days of sick leave each year they work, and it accrues. Another important benefit is called Extended Sick Leave, which is good for up to five months of leave, or one academic semester. This provision allows for leave "after the exhaustion of accumulated sick leave. . . . The amount deducted from the salary due him after the exhaustion of accumulated sick leave . . . shall not exceed the sum which is actually paid a temporary employee employed to fill his/ her position during his/her absence or, if no temporary employee was employed, the amount which would have been paid to the temporary employee had he/she been employed" (San Bernardino Community College District, 2010a, p. 63). Thus, there is flexibility in the policy so that faculty, male or female, who need time to care for a new child may have it. Though all extended leaves have to be cleared with an immediate supervisor, Dr. Jiminez (pseudonym) finds that "the administration will work with you . . . [and I] haven't seen any problems with it. . . . There was a woman who went on a year long sabbatical right after she had a child. She did this project that was useful, so she was able to have a year at home."

Policy Meets Faculty

Hearing the harrowing stories of faculty trying to manage having and raising children, one thinks of Blanche DuBois in A *Street Car Named Desire* by Tennessee Williams. Blanche, like many of the faculty we interviewed, relies on the kindness of strangers. Institutional support has to be individually negotiated with department chairs and deans, rendering institutional practices inherently capricious. A lack of codification makes those faculty who ask for leave or tenure-clock stoppage feel as if they are asking for special treatment. Others, like Professor Ingrahm, who engages in parenthood without institutional support, report that by the time one does what is required to obtain tenure, one ends up a "stranger to your kids."

Lacking support required that Professor McMillan was left to her own devices when her child got sick. Thus she took her child to class in order to avoid canceling an exam for three hundred students, and promptly received a dressing-down from one of her administrators. At Michigan or Washington, she would simply call the sick-child-care provider, and she would have a licensed professional at her home to take care of her child. It would seem that, rather than chastising faculty, administrators' time would be much more productively spent finding a provider for faculty who have sick children.

Lacking policies on child leave other than FMLA, furthermore, produced dilemmas for many participants in our studies. Although their institutions granted twelve weeks of unpaid leave, it is problematic for faculty who teach within a fifteen-week semester framework. Teaching half-time is no solution because the new parent still is not able to stay home with a new child.

Instead, imagine Dr. McMillan's institution having a flexible workload policy such as the one available at Boise State whose major advantage lies in its cost-effectiveness. Boise State's policy would have allowed her to simply not teach during the first semester after she had the baby. Instead, she would have taught all of her courses the following semester, incurring no additional costs to the institution.

Having policies on the books is only part of the solution; their effective communication the other. Perhaps understanding the importance of the communication piece can be underscored with a reminder about Professor Riley, a late-career professor, who thinks academe is not compatible with being a parent. Because many people in administrative roles are culled from those in the latter stages of their careers, it is crucial that they understand the new reality for most faculty members and be aware of whatever policies and procedures their institutions may have.

In a similar vein, it is important to remember late-career Professor Green and his need for child care. He believes that many of the worries about his own children would have been alleviated with on-campus child care. In fact, he believes it "would have been wonderful." Even at the most exemplary institutions, child care is always problematic and most institutions will not be able to provide enough on-campus care to serve all faculty who need it. However, at little cost, institutions could work out arrangements with providers in their area much like is done at the University of Washington. Also, by maintaining a list of licensed providers, new parents can have resources available to them if on-campus day care is not available or not conducive to their individual situation. In addition, many institutions could consider what the University of Michigan offers by creating a referral system to local providers. Berkeley gives parents a checklist they can use to evaluate potential child care on their own. Again, these services are of little or no cost to the institution but do signal to faculty that administrators understand the reality of their lives. It is important to remember that most faculty get hired at institutions that are geographically far removed from their social or family networks; they thus lack extended family as support networks. This realization led to the creation of the babysitting coordinator position at Williams college and, for Dr. Allison and his wife, for instance, such services would have been a welcomed stress reliever. They are both assistant professors at Comprehensive University, and because they are new to the area the only time they are able to enjoy a night out alone is when the local YMCA has a parents' night. Again, for parents who have just moved to an area, a baby-sitter referral service would be an immense help.

Given these realities, we have the following recommendations.

Recommendations

Child Care

Child care is seen as vitally important by faculty members and representatives of exemplary institutions alike, but many schools struggle with adequate provisions and long waiting lists. Even exemplary institutions may not be able to provide high-quality care to all families who desire it, including faculty, post-docs, staff, and students at both the graduate and undergraduate levels, yet recommendations can be derived from the creativity with which they found ways to address chronic shortages. We recommend that:

- Colleges and universities encourage departments to acquire grants to operate on-campus child-care facilities. For instance, the psychology department may be the appropriate place to house such a program if it offers a concentration in early childhood development. Valley College acquired grants to open a center on its campus. Thus, there are only indirect costs to the institution with grants and tuition payments covering the bulk of the expense.

- Institutions work with the state to obtain funding for child care, as exemplified by the University of Washington.

- Colleges and universities create partnerships with community child-care providers and apply for small grants to give to community-based child-care providers who, in turn, allow priority access for university employees. The University of Washington serves as a model for this approach.

- A central office such as human resources or the provost's office creates a child-care resource program that provides a list of criteria for employees to use when looking for child care. For example, Boise State has a checklist that employees can use to assess the quality of potential child-care providers.

- Appropriate personnel or department creates a babysitting coordinator who connects employees with students looking for this type of work.

- On-campus child-care facilities create flexible part-time openings that allow faculty with different schedules to utilize the high-quality child-care facilities available on campus.

- The appropriate department or office creates a resource for employees with sick children. For instance, the University of Michigan offers "Kids Kare" and UC Berkeley the "Wheezles and Sneezles" program, both of which provide a resource for employees with sick children who cannot go to their regular child care or school. The cost is minimal to the institution as parents carry the cost of the provider, and there are many at-home care companies that have opened as more and more seniors wish to stay in their homes. These types of organizations would be appropriate partners for institutions looking to create a resource for employees with sick children.

Child Leave

Pregnancy, childbirth, and adoption are major life events that increasingly affect both women's and men's careers. To ease parents' transitions into a new life phase and new responsibilities, we recommend that:

- Child-leave policies are made available to both men and women in order to avoid possible disadvantages on the basis of gender, stigmatization of women, but also to give new fathers the opportunity to care for newborns.

- Faculty are allowed to accrue sick leave that can be used for child care, a policy in place at Valley College.

- Faculty have flexibility in scheduling so that teaching responsibilities can be front or back loaded. For instance, Boise State allows faculty to move all teaching requirements to one semester so that it is possible to stay at home during the other semester (or leave town to care for an elder family member, for example).

- Colleges and universities offer a reduced teaching load the semester during which a new child enters the household either through birth or adoption.

- Institutions provide or create, as the UC system does, a short-term disability policy that will permit four months (one semester) of child care leave.

- Universities and colleges, acknowledging the unique aspects of faculty work, provide a series of options that allow for flexibility. For instance, Williams College enables faculty to take one semester off at 3/4 pay or take a one-course reduction in teaching at full pay.

- Universities and colleges reduce the pay of faculty who go on child leave only by the amount it costs the institution to hire adjunct faculty to cover their classes.

4

Thriving in Academe

Male and female faculty members differ markedly in their responses to questions about how they, overall, see their ability to balance professional and personal parts of their lives (for more detail see Appendix A: Additional Findings from the Men's Study). Though men at *all* career stages characterize their balances as working well, only late-career women sound similarly positive. Nevertheless, regardless of gender and career stage, we found examples of faculty thriving in academe, and were curious to learn more about factors that helped them do so.

As will become clear when we look more closely at these factors, the vast majority rest either on built-in characteristics of the academic profession or attitudes and behaviors of individuals, including the ingenuity of the faculty members themselves and caring acts of colleagues, mentors, administrators, partners, family, and friends. Institutional policies and programs, while existent, only minimally support faculty balancing. They make significant differences in some cases, however, and therefore deserve attention.

Inherent Factors

When asked to account for what makes their balancing acts successful, male faculty explain that their passion for what they do positively affects family life. The nature of faculty work, its inherent freedom and flexibility, is emphasized. The intensity with which the men rave about their jobs was impressive; they call the academic life "wonderful," "desirable," "a great gig," and "splendid," a finding resonating with research by Jacobs and Winslow (2004) who reported overall job satisfaction among faculty as quite high. Female faculty also mention flexibility as enabling, but only those at the late-career stage are able to fully capitalize on it. Late-career women choose, for example, whether they want the boundaries between their personal and professional spheres to be permeable or rigid, and they portray their balancing in terms equally as glowing as those used by the men across career stages. Their current situations are described as suiting "very well," "a delightful position to be in," and "much easier, much happier." To reiterate, female faculty at earlier career stages do not sound as positive when asked to describe their work-life balancing in broad strokes but they, too, share supporting factors.

Professors across career stage and gender benefit from the flexible nature of academic work allowing them to share the care of children with their partners, being "home at key times," and attending to personal needs that arise. They also are able to do work at home or at the office, further alleviating tensions between different spheres of their lives. The "lack of a true evaluation structure for professors" is quoted as enabling and "the lack of someone looking over your shoulder at every moment arguably tends to enable people to have a work-life balance." For some, academe also offers "summers off and generous amounts of breaks." Other institutional enablers matter, including reasonable expectations for faculty not to be expected to "entertain the students" or to "be able to attend every faculty meeting."

Colleagues

Upon closer analysis of enabling forces in their professional spheres of life, however, it became obvious that, first and foremost, individual colleagues, administrators, and mentors help faculty members thrive. Though many dual-career faculty face considerable challenges (see Chapter Two), there are those who encountered an understanding culture within departments. Remembering, for example, his efforts to juggle career and family obligations, midcareer Professor Eggleston reports that he and his wife received a lot of cooperation from schedule makers. It also helped, he says, that his colleagues expressed an attitude somewhere between "indifference and support as opposed to some sort of disdain" about bringing children into the office. Dr. Moller at Flagship describes a "critical mass of people with children" in her department, a fact that fosters an "understanding of what it means to have children and what you can and can't do when you have children."

Along similar lines, instructor Ehrenreich recounts how people accommodated a pregnant faculty member's schedule and covered classes and committee assignments. Also, supportive colleagues and students helped her get through difficult times when her husband had a stroke. Late-career Professor Amici, who defines her life primarily around her work, sees her department as enabling, calling it "absolutely wonderful to me. It has given me all the support and all of the acknowledgment that I needed to feel fulfilled, and all of the opportunities to do the things I wanted to do."

Late-career Ms. Monet credits her department as an enabler as well; during the times she had to take care of her aging parents out-of-state and miss several days of teaching, her colleagues covered for her so that classes did not have to be cancelled. Associate Professor Ashcroft calls his dean "the wind under my sails," convinced that he could not have accomplished all he did without him. "He set me up, but in setting me up to be positioned to do certain things, I then had early entrée into committees and boards. He would send me places to get special grooming." Dr. Dennison credits his chair for urging him to make use of university policy and stop the tenure clock after the birth of his twins. He tells the story of how he was "sort of frantic to make tenure and [the chair] was the one who said 'hey, wait a minute, what's going on in your house, let's think about this.' And it had absolutely never occurred to me that I was eligible for [leave]."

Dr. Ingrahm believes that having the same boss in his department for twenty-five years who ran an extremely amicable and collegial department made "a terrific difference," while Mr. Richardson praises his supportive boss and his institution for helping him pay for the course required to finish his Ph.D.

Support mechanisms of a bygone era are also mentioned; for instance the "great black father" fondly remembered by Dr. Jellig at HBCU. For several decades during the second part of the twentieth century, the president of his institution helped construct a climate of support that was less formal than it might be today. This is how he describes the differences between the past and the present:

> And I remember some interesting things about how this school was run. Like, we didn't have a Faculty Senate, for example, during [the president's] era. And I can remember that if people had problems, I remember one case of somebody getting sick and having some problems very early in the school year, like maybe it was say October. And I remember different ones of us taking their classes. Because I know one semester I think I had twenty-one hours and five or six preparations. . . . And that was just normally done. So I think that was the big difference, maybe, was the fact that we were pretty close to being one happy family. . . . It wasn't a case where I would say "Hey, I want to volunteer," but it was always a case where somebody was going to be out, and so you're going to have to cover their class. . . . I just remember everyone just doing it. And it was very surprising to me that when [the next president] came and then they started talking about having a Faculty Senate and they started talking about a concept of having so many sick leave days, and all this was really to me kind of new. And I remember . . . it just didn't seem right for people saying that I have to know how many sick leave days I'm going to have, how many of

these. . . . Because before, if something came up, you just told the department chair or [the president's] office, and you went and did it. . . . So, and here I think everybody pretty much understood kind of everybody, and kind of in a sense looked out for everybody.

Midcareer Professor Pryzinski credits colleagues with whom she coauthored and collaborated, as well as "fantastic mentors" as major enablers. She remembers one person telling her that "the best way to be an academic is to be so good that everybody just leaves you alone." Following that advice, she became "so good at what I do, that no one picks on me, you know what I mean. Everyone just leaves me alone. I think that's an enabler because I'm not being picked at, I'm not a subject of judgment all the time." When people leave you alone because of your excellence, she explains, you have the "potential for balance and to open your life up to other dimensions that can work to sustain you and make you more healthy in a holistic way."

Policies

Being single after her divorce and without children, Dr. Pryzinski did not need the *same* type of support as faculty parents, but she did require help in making corrections to what she perceived as a highly imbalanced life. It was her institution's junior sabbatical that enabled her to do so. "It was just like the university went 'boop, okay, you're over there now. You don't have to be in this space for one semester.'" It felt to her as if the college was sending her the message that, as a junior untenured professor, they wanted her to figure out how to bring more of her research to publication and how to create a sustainable future for herself at the institution. The junior sabbatical, she explains, was "their way of saying we want you to get tenure, and here is some extra time you can take for that very purpose."

Occasionally other policies are mentioned as supportive of faculty. Dr. Dennison, who stopped his tenure clock after the birth of his twins, calls parental leave policies "extremely important." Yet those policies are unpredictable and, though helping faculty deal with pregnancy and childbirth, they seem limited. Faculty at Flagship mention that a paid semester's leave is granted and the tenure clock can temporarily be stopped. However, the policy is not "official," meaning sanctioned, put in writing, advertised as part of employee benefits packages, and equally available to all. Dr. Moller at Flagship, pregnant with her second child, describes the situation as follows:

> It's not well publicized though. I couldn't find it on the web, my chair didn't know. It's something I think the deans kind of do, but it's not publicized. . . . There certainly is not [a policy] university wide. I think each school within the university might have its own policy somewhere that's not readily available. It may not be in writing.

Dr. McLeod at the same institution, also mother of a three-year-old and pregnant, corroborates:

> [Flagship] has a fairly good maternity policy but it's not like a real official policy. It's sort of an "ad-hoc" policy. . . . Most people get a research leave. They usually give us a semester off from teaching. . . . I'm not sure about [people's] knowledge because it's not on the web anywhere. . . . So I feel like if you didn't talk to anybody who'd gotten it you might not know that you can get it.

She explains that the official policy at Flagship is based on the Family and Medical Leave Act and, therefore, whether or not a woman is granted maternity leave (disguised as research leave) depends on the department. With this practice, she elaborates, the university obtains an element of flexibility and can grant faculty leave that staff members do not get. "And I'm guessing that's part of the reason there's not an official policy."

Serious equity considerations would arise should pregnant women have to take their "research leave" to have children while others use it for its intended purpose. Yet Dr. McLeod insists she is to be granted research leave again, in addition to the leave she will enjoy after her baby's birth. Though limited, child leave policies do play a role in helping faculty thrive.

A faculty member at Community College describes how his institution grants flexible schedules for family reasons. "I think we're real flexible around here, and we're very supportive of faculty and staff in terms of liberal leave policies and that sort of thing if you have situations with your children and you need to attend to them, we are cognizant of that. We realize that people have lives outside of this institution." A junior faculty member at Private Comprehensive credits her encouraging colleagues who extended her tenure clock without question, rearranged classes to accommodate her leave, and even gave her a baby shower, an important symbolic gesture of their support. She is happy to be able to take her baby to work:

> The work environment is also very enabling because I bring the baby to work with me. I go in a few hours a week here and there to meet with students who are doing research with me. . . . I'm not working anywhere near full-time but I'm trying to keep my foot in the door and be a presence in my office. So I just bring the baby with me. I strap her in a carrier, and nobody bats an eye about the fact that I'm working with the baby strapped to my body.

Dr. Carver consciously chose not to join the faculty at an Ivy League or Research One university that would have higher publishing and grant writing standards. She did that "for the sake of work-life balance" and is happy about her choice. She is of the opinion that her work environment ought to be standard in academia, and if she had a nonacademic job, things would be more difficult to manage. She marvels at the flexibility of both her work and her husband's schedule and wonders "how women with nonacademic jobs manage and do motherhood."

Culture

Faculty in both the women's and men' studies mention institutional support that helps them thrive, yet more often it falls to colleagues to enable faculty on an ad hoc basis to tend to personal needs. Late-career Professor Riley, for instance, points out that his department covers for female faculty who are pregnant and have young kids, but it is up to the department to figure out how to do it. Though his institution has leave policies on the books, he reports "we don't get to hire anyone to replace these people who are on leave for various reasons." The burden of filling in for a faculty member on leave, in other words, is shouldered by those remaining. Institutional readiness for situations necessitating faculty leave is lacking, and faculty thrive largely due to the efforts of individuals who, collectively, build a supportive culture.

Senior Professor Adela claims that his college views itself as a family, a notion defining the dynamics of its environment. Junior Professor Williams credits the culture of his small liberal arts college as enabling to his life balance. Reasonable expectations allow him to evenly divide his time between teaching and research. His daily routines, and his stress level, differ significantly from those of his pre-tenure colleagues at research-intensive institutions, and his descriptions of those differences are worth quoting at length:

> The young professors, when we were brought in, it's been emphasized what the administration wants in order

for us to get tenure, and in order for us to be viewed as successful professors. . . . It's emphasized that they want us to spend about half of our time on research and about half of our time on teaching. And my friends who are at research-intensive universities, R1 places, have a very different focus. They're much more research oriented, and it's clear to me when I talk to them that their tenure or their success is going to be determined solely by their research, and it really has very little to do with how well the teaching goes, at least at the under-graduate level. . . . So it's forced on them that their focus is completely research, they spend all their time doing research. They spend time trying to get their gradu-ate students to do as much research as possible. . . . So, when we were in graduate school . . . you were encour-aged both negatively and positively to work as many hours as you possibly could. Everyone worked six days a week, and probably fifty percent of the people I was in graduate school with worked seven days a week. And it was all to get this research because for us, the impetus at the time as students was our PhD thesis. . . . So the faster you got the results that went in your thesis, the faster you could graduate and move on with the rest of your life. The impetus for the professor was, if it was a young professor, the professor needed those research pub-lications to get tenure. If it was an older professor, then it was prestige. So my friends who became young profes-sors at research institutions are sort of perpetuating this model by having the same attitudes with their students that we had when we were graduate students. At a place like this where there are no graduate students, it's pretty impossible to carry on that type of mindset. So there's really nothing you can do to force an undergraduate to do research in a lab, because while that would be great

for me if a research undergraduate worked 60 hours a
week, in reality it has no bearing on whether that student graduates in four years, which is all they really care
about. So for me, it's taken a lot of stress out of my job,
because I don't have to push my students. I don't have
to worry about threatening my relationship with my students. And at the end of the day I can go home and say
well, as long as I'm doing a good job with my teaching,
my job is going to be secure. And the feedback I've
gotten from student reviews has been positive as far as
my teaching goes. So I'm not too worried about that.
But I think that kind of situation makes it a lot easier
for me to survive mentally.

Assistant Professor Trenton at the same university (though in
a different department) echoes his colleague's take on differences
in cultures and expectations across institutions. He describes the
peer culture where he works as "healthy" in comparison with
the Ivy League university with its many "workaholics" where he
received his degree. Now the message he gets is "they want you
to spend time with your family, and it's legitimate too, to do that.
And they want you to do things not related to academia. . . .
If I'm not here on a Saturday afternoon . . . nobody's going to
make me feel bad." Along the same lines, Dr. Hall appreciates
being able not to "let work just eat my entire life." He explains
that Community College does not expect him to "publish a book
every so often, and articles, or I get fired. So that's nice. So I can
completely veg out if I need to." Dr. Thomas likes working at
Community College as well, finding the small size of the institution inherently enabling: "I think the smaller the program, the
smaller the college, there's a little more flexibility to try to help
out with young families, and academics who have young families,
I would hope, in good departments."

Resources

Resources of various types help faculty thrive; one participant describes how his college's ample resources benefit faculty by providing sufficient research and clerical support. In addition, he values the presence of slightly older faculty members with children who are able to help him find a good child-care situation.

Technology is mentioned as enabling good balance; distance learning, for instance, helps faculty to spend more time at home or, as in the case of Mr. Thompson at Community College, pursue his Ph.D. online while working full-time. Dr. Molina at the same institution views technology as "definitely an enabler.... I'm able to be sociable by e-mail in the middle of the night with students and with faculty in ways that I never would have been able to ten years ago." Dr. Lilian agrees; technology, in the view of the thirty-four-year-old, allows for a fast-paced life and successful integration. She draws comparisons across generations. Hers, she thinks, enjoys a distinct advantage over previous ones because its members have grown up with technology and a fast pace, both of which make it relatively easy for them to meet the demands of modern life. Older persons may have to adapt, but "for me, this is how you operate," she says. Whereas her mother's life was neatly divided into work and family time, telecommunication makes it possible for Dr. Lilian to bring work home. Though some may consider the development disadvantageous, Dr. Lilian thinks "it just depends on what kind of person you are." And for her, doing several things at once, mixing the personal and the professional, and constantly being on the move is not a problem but simply a way of life. Multitasking helps her manage her busy life as a successful professional and single mother.

> Having an only child, I found that after 9 o'clock I am very productive because at 9 o'clock she is in bed, and I'm not tired and ready to crash myself.... I can be

doing a load of laundry, watching television and reading e-mail all at the same time. . . . And I'm content. I don't feel like I'm burdened to be sitting there reading these e-mails. I'm watching my favorite TV show, I have on my favorite slippers, in about an hour you hear the drier "ding," which is fine. I'm doing things that I need to do. What's stressful is if I couldn't do these things, and they'd pile up on me. That's when the stress comes in but as long as I can keep moving and get things done, I'm fine.

The practices described above are called "hyper-planning" by another faculty member, and though they work for Dr. Lilian, they extract costs and entail sacrifices, as discussed further in Appendix B (see the section "Challenge and Sacrifice").

Time, a strong record, and professional experience help faculty thrive once they have advanced on the career ladder. The following are selected quotes illustrating this point of view:

- "The fact that I've been successful, you know, I'm a good teacher, I do research, I bring in gobs of money, I do service, basically has allowed me to be very selective of what I do and who I want to work with."

- "You're finally into it. You know, you're tenured, you're a full professor, you kind of know the game, you can do it."

- "Experience is a big enabler."

- "I think we're getting better at balancing our lives as we get older. . . . Perhaps we become more focused on what we need to do. . . . Perhaps it's also an improved skill level of making right judgments, and knowing when to stop something and go do something else that you need to do."

- "I've learned how to turn down things that are flattering when I think about them, and think this is just going to be more stress."

- "I think there is also just an acceptance of me. That I am who I am. I always knew that but I think I used to feel a lot more cocky about it. Then I went through a very insecure period about it, and now it is 'que sera'; it is the way I am. . . . It is wonderful."

- "As I see it, my career has gotten easier and easier the closer I get to retirement. . . . Things seem to be click-ing into place, and I seem to have found my niche and my abilities seem to match my position, and there is a certain amount of success. And things seem to be fall-ing into place at this late point in the career."

Retired Professor Metzger tells stories about "eccentricity credits" he accumulated over time, and how those were helpful in allowing him to craft his life as he saw fit. "I think one thing was that you had to be skillful at some of the things that were highly valued in that particular culture. . . . If you did some of the things really well that were valued in that culture, then you could get away with some things people didn't understand. They'd give you a good break on the explanation of it, because you were good at this other stuff, so it must be okay." One example he gives involves "strange grade schemes" such as giving final exams only two weeks into the semester; another pertains to his choice of dress: "A onetime dean used to be very annoyed with me because I didn't dress right. . . . But the fact was, I could build eccentric-ity credits with my consulting there, because I was valued in that culture . . . so they wouldn't say anything about . . . the way I was dressed." He concludes: "I always did what I wanted." Dr. Jellig echoes the sentiment and reports that being perceived as "kind of weird" has been enabling to him because "I was able to pretty much kind of do what I wanted to do, and no one really kind of bothered me."

Midcareer Professor Pelletier talks about cultivating "the skill of having a very controlled and very targeted meltdown" in order to achieve her goals. Yet she warns that "throwing your weight around" requires a certain standing, and it has to be done very carefully, and if you do it too many times, "it ceases to be effective and people do think you're crazy."

More directly related to the work-life relationship, midcareer Professor Dotolo provides detail about how being at an advanced career stage helps his balancing act:

> I'm older, I'm further in my career. I can say "no" to more things. We have more money because I'm further in my career, and I don't have to do things for money; I don't have to teach summer school. You know, when I was young, they didn't pay you very much. My start-ing salary was $12,600 when I started. And you had to work summers just to make ends meet. But now I don't have to do that because I'm older, I'm more established in my career, they pay me more. So I have my summers off. And I think the summers are where, if anything gets shaky during the year because we're all working too hard with classes or school or whatnot, we always make it back in the summer, because we're completely together in the summer. We have a cabin up in the mountains. . . . Up in the mountains it's cool, and we just pick up and go, and we stay there from June until August, and it's just the family. So we feel like we pretty tightly bonded as a result of it.

These findings indicate that faculty members' sense of what they can and cannot do positively correlates with perceptions of success: once faculty have established themselves and built a

firm reputation, they can more easily "afford" to throw fits, be eccentric, embrace who they are, select what they are willing to do, and how they spend their time, including time with family. Spalter-Roth and Erskine (2005) describe a similar phenomenon. According to their research on work-life policy use among academic parents, particularly mothers, they conclude that institutional help is not treated as a needs-based entitlement but rather a reward for the most academically successful women. It is obvious that if freedom, flexibility, and support have to be earned, large segments of the faculty population, including most junior faculty, are denied such goods. They have to rely, once again, on the willingness of individuals in their lives to help them thrive.

Significant Others

Our research indeed strongly suggests that a major factor in helping faculty thrive are significant others who take care of the children and domestic chores, or simply serve as support networks. Dr. Johnson has a stay-at-home wife who helps him balance, and he does not "have to worry about a lot of the at-home kind of stuff." He stresses the difference between his life and those colleagues who are juggling dual careers, scrambling, for instance, to make child-care arrangements. "That's not something that would come up for us," he says, "because we don't have that situation."

Supportive spouses and partners come up frequently as helping faculty thrive: supportive wives who bring balance, stability, and strength to face "the rest of the stuff," who serve as a gauge and complain when life is out of whack given that, otherwise, "it's hard to know that you're out of whack." Wives who are flexible and understanding, care only about helping the family, thus being "an enabler par excellence" or "a homebody . . . not biting at the bit like some women wanting to get out and start a career." One person says that "a great deal of credit goes to my wife. Although she's not very pleased with the fact that I spend so much time away from home, she has taken on a tremendous amount of responsibility in terms of raising the kids," and another considers himself "blessed because Keith is a great cook and does a lot of domestic chores."

Dr. Mahoney at Public Comprehensive characterizes his relationship as "the thing that allows the career" and provides detail into what makes a truly supportive partner who understands the life of an academic and is, what he calls, "low maintenance."

> I have the support of my partner. And she's not the workaholic I am, but since she has her own professional career, and she has her own degrees, and I think she understands what goes on. But she's the kind of person that if she won the lottery, she'd quit working. If I won the lottery, I'd probably keep working. But I'd probably still want to do the kind of things that I'm doing right now. So I guess that's the distinction. So she's very supportive as far as time and so forth. Because I've had colleagues whose wives, either they don't work or they have like a very blue collar vision of work, and work is what happens between nine and five, and when you come home you're not working, or the other aspect, if you're sitting in front of the computer that's not work, that's screwing around. Working is swinging hammers and getting sweaty and things like that. And I know that they have found it very difficult because certainly as an untenured professor, and a lot of times you are just sitting there staring at the screen going God, I don't know what the heck to do. That actually does count as work. Sometimes you work on the really productive hours and days where you just nail everything, and I'm like wow, if I could have a month of those days, I'd just rule the world. But the truth is those days are really the fruition of a lot of sort of staring at the sky, or the computer,

and then it just comes. So she understands the notion of what exactly is my work, and sometimes I make dinner, go back to work or something, or see if there's anything that she really wants.

Participants in the women's study often portray their spouses and partners in similarly positive ways. Dr. Sutherland calls her stay-at-home husband "without a doubt the most important enabler" while others refer to their husbands as wonderfully supportive, like-minded and compatible, working well together, being of enormous help, enabling her to focus on her work, or at least being "not as demanding" and "OK with me going all over the world. That's an enabler."

Investing in a healthy relationship serves, among other things, a utilitarian purpose. Because work comes first in Assistant Professor Mahoney's life, he seeks to keep his personal relationship healthy so it does not interfere with work. "I try to invest in a relationship to keep it healthy," he says, "because if the relationship is healthy I'm free to focus on work, right? . . . [H]aving been divorced and learning from experiences there, I realized that you have to preemptively do things to try and maintain the relationship and not wait."

In addition to spouses and partners, simply having a family and being actively engaged in it help faculty thrive: full Professor Dotolo has two teenage children, and he and his wife always made sure to not rigidly divide roles. They stay flexible, he says, and that is good because he cannot excuse himself from domestic chores and just concentrate exclusively on his work. The university will "suck you in," he says, and if you were freed from some of these domestic tasks for a long period of time, you would never do them, and that would draw you too much into your work. "And you wouldn't have any way to get back into the family process." Similarly, Dr. Moller remains sane because of her daughter, who "laughs and you laugh, and for a couple of hours at least before bedtime I can most days put work aside and not think about it. I think that's good for me."

Extended family and networks also helps faculty thrive: in-laws provide child care, and friends, support groups, and family help, listen, and serve as sounding boards. "We come from large families, both my wife and I. So without that network of support, I don't think we could have done it," is how Dr. Zavella puts it.

Participants in the women's study emphasize the importance of "sister circles" and other forms of women's support groups as essential to their thriving in academe. Professor Beseley, for instance, finds the academic community as potentially very alienating for women because of its supervisory and administrative nature, male orientation, and male domination. Therefore, she says:

> One thing I try to do, since I have been doing this for about thirty years, I really try to talk with . . . any new female who joins my department or close department. I make a connection with that person to say "you won't find this in the handbook, but I know that you can do this." . . . So I think sister circles are important for women.

Late-career Dr. Kasper finds that, although men have helped her as well, "having women at various points in my career is absolutely key." She continues to interact with female colleagues outside of academe as well, emphasizing that "having women around is very important. . . . Particularly enabling," she says, is a mixture of social and professional camaraderie.

Senior Professor Posen describes as well how female support helped her deal with many things, some of them particularly relevant to women of her age group, such as menopause.

> I think [menopause] is starting to have an impact on how I feel, and you do bring that to the work place.

The positive thing is that our front office staff is heavily female, and there is a great relationship between the female faculty and the female staff in our department. On the whole, it is a very comfortable, friendly atmosphere. So there is that kind of sharing of those of us in our fifties with the younger women, about meno-pause stories, that kind of thing. . . . We are very close. There isn't that kind of separation between staff and faculty that you see in other departments or places. So, people bring their children in. . . . Children, dogs. So I think that helps, to be in a fairly positive atmosphere in the workplace.

Although older generations of men do not mention male sup-port groups, Dr. Trenton says that at his institution young male academics who have children, especially those with tenure, are trying to support each other. "They talk about how it's going, trade suggestions and things like that. That's very informal but it's valuable."

The definition of enablers is not restricted to what is avail-able to faculty to help them balance, such as supportive spouses, family, and colleagues, but also extends to what is *not* there. Listed are the absence of a life partner ("things are easy for me because I'm unmarried, I don't have a significant other"), being an empty nester ("now our lives revolve around our professional pursuits," "my children are in their twenties or thirties, and they don't require the constant necessity of my time"), or a combination of the two: "For me, by everyone being grown and me not having a spouse, that has enabled me to make decisions independent of what somebody else would want you to say or do. . . . Because my children are grown, and my husband is deceased, I have control over my life in comparison to someone who perhaps does not."

Choosing not to have children in the first place but to remain child-free instead helps some faculty thrive. Life is less complicated without children ("you don't have to deal with soccer practice"), and not having children keeps expenses down. As Dr. Mahoney explains, having money, in turn, allows him to hire out jobs around the house he either does not feel capable of doing or does not enjoy. Dr. Zavella echoes the sentiment: "Having more money and now, more freedom. I actually just put the dog in a kennel, and we can go away for a weekend. And we do that . . . we're just taking every advantage that we can. . . . My wife has the ability of adjusting her schedule, my daughters are in college . . ." Not being bogged down by expectations generated by the extended family also helps balance life, as Dr. Jellig explains: "We weren't caught up in that thing where we had to be with grandpa on this particular date. Because that's what some of my friends would say, they would have to spend Thanksgiving this year with their mother's family, and Christmas with the father's family. Then they would have to go Easter with this other family. We never really had that, you know, and I think that was the main thing, that we didn't have those we were locked into."

Faculty Ingenuity

Above and beyond external forces, faculty resort to their own ingenuity and a wealth of coping strategies in order to thrive (for greater detail see the women's study, which devotes entire sections to faculty coping). Included are multitasking, exercise, enjoying the outdoors to "get grounded," and refueling through hobbies and personal pleasures. There is talk about spirituality and prayer as a way to refocus the mind on the purpose of the profession and the people who might benefit from one's work. Faculty members work on "being positive," seeing opportunities, and downplaying negative parts of life. One can always work on one's attitude reminds midcareer Professor Hanson, whose motto is "quit whining" and reminding himself that, in comparison to previous generations, he is relatively well off. Historically, he says, "people didn't have a work-life balance; you just did what you did. And it wasn't a balance, it was just I'll spend the time that I can spend with my kids, and that's fine. I'm in the factory, and when I get off, I get off, and that's pretty much all there is to it. So part of it is recognizing that even on days when there appears to be no leisure. . . . In the grand scheme of things, it's not going to kill me."

Midcareer Professor Molina at Community College also reports "taking the long view." He says he does not understand couples who are "always kind of looking for the next big score professionally, and they're moving around a lot, even with kids." He tends to be conservative, he says, and advocates that "you make a home wherever you end up." So he and his wife are determined to make the most of their city of residence and the institutions where they work. "That whole idea of not thinking that there's going to be some kind of impending change on the horizon helps. That's an enabler to my mind because it enables you to be more patient on a day-to-day basis about certain things, it gives you more perspective." Over time Dr. Molina has become an increasingly spiritual person, something that has made him "a lot more philosophical about making the most of this life, and defining that as a whole lot less about what I accomplish in the profession." Ironically, he reports, he has become more productive in traditionally defined ways. "That's an irony," he says. "I've really kind of ratcheted down how much I really kind of value or define myself as a success or failure through professionalism, and yet I've become more professionally active."

Dr. Ingrahm finds it enabling that he does not have much ambition, while his colleague Sneed adjusts his attitude by "getting control of my ego." It helps him that he does not "much care, and never has much cared, what people think that I should do." Given the ever-increasing demands emanating from the university, at some point, if you're healthy enough, he comments, "you just say 'no.'" He learned over time to put himself into a position where he felt good about himself professionally, "still be above average, and be okay with not being a superstar."

His junior colleague Ionesco reports the opposite. Drive and ambition, commitment, dedication, and just wanting to get things done keep him going. Dr. Jellig benefited from always assuming that he would be successful and "that I was supposed to do what I wanted to do." Having goals and objectives, and deadlines for when he needs to meet them, helps him cope with obstacles, reports Assistant Professor Johnson.

Assistant Professor McLeod finds it helpful to remind herself that, because she has a family, she can not afford to go off on tangents, but needs to use her time efficiently. She states: "You're a little more focused because you realize you have constraints." She also embraces the idea of dedicating certain times to doing things that easily become distracting if allowed to penetrate the entire day. Her example is reading e-mail only during a child's swim practice, and otherwise "not touching it," thereby freeing up the limited time she has to be productive.

Ms. Ohler makes lists. Carrying around her calendar and her "little notebook," she finds it essential to keep lists and thereby keeping herself organized. Dr. Allison, father of two young children, copes by being organized, planning well, and coordinating schedules with his wife. It helps him to have a certain amount of flexibility, he says, not just in terms of his work environment but also mentally so he can "try to take it as it comes." Having children precludes being rigid, according to him; life is unpredictable and flexibility is necessary. "So if there's a day when you thought you were going to get some stuff done, you know you just work on trying to make up for that work some other time, once you put the kids to bed or waking up early the next morning. . . . When I was doing my dissertation, I used to get up at 4:30 in the morning. . . . I was tired a lot, but that's the way I got it finished." His colleague Ampofo sounds similar. He and his wife communicate about schedules so they can take turns taking care of their children. "We plan ahead," he says, and "try to understand each other's plan."

While some professors use structure to get a grip on too much work and too many demands, retired Professor Metzger finds himself in a different situation. He needed to introduce structure into his life in order to work and feel productive now that his life is devoid of institutional demands. There is plenty of good advice in the old time-management literature from the 1970s, he says, explaining how he copes by setting time and schedule periods for writing, making sure the phone is turned off and other interruptions are prevented. It also helps him to have carved out a space whose sole designation is work. "Get yourself a place to work on what your work is, and don't do anything else there." Self-discipline also helps faculty member Richardson, who uses his "anal retentive foundations" as a coping strategy, straightening his desk, organizing, and getting stuff done in advance to avoid anxiety or pressure.

On the other side of the spectrum is first-year Assistant Professor Hall, who copes by not stressing out about things as much as others he knows. He says: "I tend to be kind of laid back. . . . I know a lot of people who are sort of driven into nervous fits by the prospect of taking their oral exams, for example." Not stressing out works for Assistant Professor Mahoney as well, specifically when it means ignoring, for the sake of sanity, work that needs to be done around the house. "And so my partner and I joke," he says, "because . . . there's a limit to the number of hours in the day, and so our house is not very clean, and so we joke we need a wife, and then we joke we need a husband as well. Even though she does the repairs, there's a whole list of things that need repairs, and it's excruciatingly long. And so we tend to be lazy."

Others set limits in different ways. Dr. Jankovich limits the amount of work he takes home, saying: "I don't want to be a workaholic at home because then I end up hibernating in my little room there. I wouldn't want to do that." His colleague Dr. Trenton used to try to meet everybody's needs during his first year, but then found himself "a little harder to reach" in order to get done what he needed to. He guards against becoming a "super nerd type" and spends relatively much time outside of academe, knowing full well "I'm not going to end up at Princeton or wherever." He would not trade his relatively balanced life for a more intense career.

Another example of a refined coping system is personified by Dr. Lilian, who masterfully integrates various aspects of her life. She invites her family along on business trips, for example, and while she attends meetings they go sightseeing. Everybody has dinner together, however. She recalls a recent trip: "Just knowing that they were there, and knowing that they were in the hotel . . . that was fun."

Integration is also used as a coping strategy by Dr. McMillan, who employs it primarily to prevent isolation and stress in her professional life. Specifically, she collaborates with people in other departments, reaching out and making connections with scholars who do similar work. She remembers realizing that "I have to be the one to make those connections to allow this thing that I do to work." She describes doing a small study with a colleague at a neighboring college as a "tremendous lift."

> So now I remove myself from my workplace almost every Friday . . . and we work all day. . . . We can off-load our stuff on each other, then we jump into our work. That is just like the most "wow" thing for me.

Junior faculty member Landers talks about how his race and age serve as inherently enabling factors for him: "Another enabler is that frankly because I was young and African American, I was not going to be a failure. I don't know if you understand that, but that was an enabler, just that itself. I'm not going to be the loose chain or whatnot. . . . When I first started here I had a lot of students come up to me and say 'wow, they finally did it' [meaning, hired a person of color]. And I just didn't want to be the person who . . . couldn't hack it."

In conclusion, much helps the faculty members in our studies thrive and, undeniably, many forces aid them in their efforts to lead balanced lives. Whatever success they have doing so does not emanate from a vacuum, nor is it attributable solely to individual strengths and attributes that they, personally, might possess, impressive though their coping strategies are. Many are surrounded, in short, by a multitude of enablers.

First and foremost, individual persons help faculty thrive, both in their personal and professional realms. Included are colleagues, mentors, administrators, spouses, partners, children, extended family members, friends, and networks. And though the impact of institutional policies and programs pales in comparison to that of individual persons, some institutional factors are mentioned as helping faculty thrive. For one, the collective acts of individuals produce cultures conducive to faculty thriving, whether or not family-friendly policies and programs are in place. A theme emerging in both studies was that of departments or colleges constructing cultures of support, "family cultures," that help faculty deal with challenging situations. Examples include relatively sane productivity expectations at a liberal arts college allowing for richer personal lives than elite research institutions allow. The institutional self-image as a family makes it possible for some faculty to thrive because they experience accommodations of needs deriving from demanding personal situations. Colleagues teach classes for faculty on leave, for instance, and schedule makers take into account the needs of dual-career couples as well as parents. People do not object to children being brought to the office and envelop faculty in a climate that feels supportive and generous.

These cultural constructions matter greatly, but they are not enough. Faculty thriving cannot be left to the luck of the draw: those who happen to find themselves in a supportive culture have a chance at balancing their lives, those who don't must fend for themselves. In addition, it seems hardly fair to the caring colleagues who pick up the slack for those who need accommodations. Clearly, reliable structures have to exist that support faculty in thriving above and beyond what well-meaning individuals are willing and able to do for their colleagues. And we did find some of those structural provisions. Examples include junior sabbaticals to increase not only scholarly productivity but also provide for a healthier, more balanced approach to life. Stoppage of the tenure clock, as controversial as the policy is, enables some faculty to take care of newborns, and child leave was granted to faculty members in the women's study. Yet and still, we argue that these policies fall short of what is needed. For one, they were not granted consistently, not by all institutions involved in our studies, and they are neither innovative nor far-reaching enough to effectively support faculty thriving. Therefore, faculty relied heavily on their own devices.

They developed an arsenal of powerful coping strategies to deal with obstacles. Those included, among many others, attitudinal "adjustments," regenerative behaviors (hobbies, pastime activities), and relationship management that allowed for maximum efficiency balancing work and life. It could be argued that anyone, regardless of how supportive one's workplace, needs coping strategies to balance life. Though this is true, we believe that the degree to which the participants in our research, particularly in the women's study and the younger generations of men, had to rely on their own strategies to cope is worrisome. They were, at best, able to construct fragile systems to deal with life challenges, and we know, based on the testimony of the late-career women in particular, that those systems are prone to break down, and that many sacrifices were made along the way. Therefore, even at the conclusion of a chapter on "faculty thriving," we reiterate the central message of this book: institutional renewal to support faculty thriving is paramount; and it is possible to do so, as the exemplary colleges and universities showcased in this study illustrate.

5

Summary and Conclusions

During the coverage of Barack Obama's inauguration as 44th president of the United States, MSNBC commentator Rachel Maddow pointed out how calm Obama's demeanor had been, both during inauguration events and during the years leading up to them. She has seen him tear up only twice, she said, once talking about the death of his grandmother, and the second time when he mentioned his regrets for not having been able to spend more time with his daughters during his campaign.

We as a society exact a heavy price not just from women but from men as well who, past and present alike, are often asked to work brutal hours and thus forfeit any semblance of a healthy balance between personal and professional spheres. Lopsided lives, in turn, entail costs and sacrifices.

To be sure, the relationships between people's personal and professional lives are not exclusively defined by their work and their family situations. Scholars and practitioners are increasingly realizing that "workplaces and families are embedded in the communities in which they are located" (Voydanoff, 2005, p. 583). Bookman (2004, as cited in Voydanoff, 2005, p. 593) developed a family-friendly community index including economic self-sufficiency, housing affordability, child care, elder care, public libraries, public safety and transportation, parks and open spaces, for instance, and it is easy to see how the presence or absence of these affect how well people might be able to balance. Given that the workplace is not the only domain shaping people's lives, one might ask why it should have any role in facilitating people's balancing acts. Answers to this question come easily.

Colleges and universities, for one, are intended to be places where new knowledge is sought, and they are meant to generate life-altering insights that ultimately improve people's lives. Such knowledge is neither exclusively created in laboratories nor in the professor's study. It is also derived from lived experience, and for that reason institutions of higher education are well positioned to serve as social laboratories where cutting edge policies are tried and tested. Those policies might well make people not just happier, and happiness is an essential human aspiration (Noddings, 2003), but also more productive, if one wants to apply human capital theory. By adopting and implementing such policies, universities and colleges would no longer lose talented people who are significant investments, nor would they need to worry about clogged recruiting pipelines caused by their inability to compete with more family-friendly workplaces. They would not lose the talented scholar whose partner was not accommodated, nor would they lose the nationally known researcher who could not see herself on a campus without child care, leave policies, and career flexibility. Neither would they see the productivity rate of their accomplished faculty drop because there is no assistance with elder and family care, and they would not put end-of-career faculty into awkward positions because there is no flexible retirement plan. Institutions of higher education are part of a larger community, in short, and well positioned to serve as examples of what is possible. Sullivan, Hollenshead, and Smith (2004) quote an associate provost at a research university: "We do things to keep our faculty. As more women move into faculty ranks, family issues come to the fore and we respond to them. . . . Societal influences demand [work-family policies]" (p. 25).

According to Gappa and others (2007, p. 322), American colleges and universities have undergone significant changes over the last few decades, resulting in both a workplace and workforce different in many ways from how they used to be. Yet, as the authors point out, many institutions of higher education have been slow to adapt their programs and policies accordingly. They continue to expect faculty, for instance, to operate like the "ideal worker" of a bygone era, one who had few responsibilities besides professional ones.

Most of the faculty members whose stories are included in this book attest to the points made earlier. Their institutions—which include a range of missions, charters, sizes, traditions, and budgetary means—provide only minimal support for them to meet the various challenges that derive from *not* being an ideal worker. And many younger faculty, male and female alike, no longer fall into the category of ideal worker. Instead they have serious personal commitments, be it to spouses and partners, children, or other significant people and causes in their lives.

The inclusion of diverse faculty in our research produced empirical evidence for something most academics have witnessed themselves or know at least anecdotally: times have changed from when, as late-career Professor Jackson remembers "[t]he man went off to work, and all the work was done, at home, by the lady."

We consider ourselves lucky to have been able to capture testimony like the one just quoted, rendered by late-career male faculty and obtained just in the nick of time before they retire and leave academe. Comparing their accounts of life-work balancing with those of their younger male colleagues, and female colleagues at any career stage, brings to light just how much has indeed changed. Listening to diverse groups of faculty talk, especially different generations, drove home the point that though the gender divide used to be tremendously powerful in academe, many younger men and women no longer inhabit qualitatively different spheres. As discussed in greater detail in the full-length women's study (Philipsen, 2008), late-career female faculty had horrendous stories to tell about their difficulties in gaining entrance into the profession and establishing themselves, battling chauvinism, second shifts, and overt discrimination that defy imagination. Similarly difficult to imagine today is the degree of freedom from entanglement in caregiving and domestic responsibilities that older generations of male faculty routinely enjoyed. Not so today. Listening carefully to Dr. Dennison, who struggles with being a part-time single father of twins, his story sounds remarkably similar to those of female colleagues.

There is no doubt that workload differences between male and female faculty continue to exist, a fact we do not wish to downplay. According to recent research on doctoral students, mothers spend more time on child care and housework than fathers (Mason, 2009). For the purposes of this book, however, more relevant than the differences between the genders were the similarities between men and women at the early- and midcareer stages. When younger male faculty talked to us about the challenges they encounter trying to be a good father and a good professor (Chapter Three), making dual-career relationships work (Chapter Two), and finding the time to establish relationships and have a thriving personal life (Chapters Two and Three), they echoed the concerns articulated by their female colleagues. The testimony lends additional credence to the call of those who have come before us and demanded institutional change to accommodate faculty in their quest to balance personal and professional lives. Whereas those changes used to focus on issues considered "women's issues," such as maternity leave, child care, or tenure-clock stoppage, we have made it abundantly clear that men are beginning to have as much of a stake in "family-friendly" (or as we prefer to call it, "life-friendly") policies and programs as women. It is to the issue of institutional change and renewal we therefore turned.

Going beyond simply calling for change, we provide examples of what selected institutions of higher education are pursuing to better meet the needs of their faculty, staff, and students. In Chapters One, Two, and Three, we weave together the testimony of faculty expressing their needs, teasing out the differences and similarities along the lines of gender and career stage, and discuss possible institutional responses to these needs. Placed in the context of a total of seven colleges and universities, and a variety of disciplines, faculty discuss: (a) the importance of flexibility in crafting a career (Chapter One); (b) changing definitions and lived practices surrounding divisions of labor, marriage, and partnership, and dual-career or dual-academic-career issues (Chapter Two); and (c) parenting, especially current definitions of what it means to be an engaged father (Chapter Three).

In each chapter we are not satisfied with simply stating and illustrating a problem, dwelling on a narrative of constraint (O'Meara, Terosky, & Neumann, 2008, p. 2). Instead, we introduce a narrative of growth (O'Meara, Terosky, & Neumann, 2008, p. 2) and showcase strategies employed by selected institutions to address the challenges of faculty. We speculate what would happen if "policy met faculty" and detail recommendations concerning the issues that appeared to be most pressing based on our research: career flexibility, spousal/partner hiring, child care, and child leave for men and women.

Pursuing a dialectic approach—simultaneously engaging in a focus on constraint and on growth—we added Chapter Four, the organization of which differs from the previous three. Here we produce a rich tapestry of faculty who describe how they continue to thrive, sometimes with the help of institutional support but mostly without it. Inspiring accounts are rendered not only about personal and professional support networks but also a host of creative coping strategies that faculty employ in order to be successful and, ultimately, thrive.

Although Chapter Four provides evidence of both resourcefulness and support networks many faculty members enjoy, it is neither ethically defensible nor economically smart for institutions of higher education to leave it solely to the individual to cope in the post-ideal-worker era. As Sorcinelli and Near reminded us as far back as 1989, "it is obvious . . . that no personal coping strategy, or set of them, will be adequate in themselves to solve the problems as they now exist" (Sorcinelli & Near, 1989, p. 78). They insisted that problems of what they call "negative spillover between work and personal life" cannot simply be solved through individual dedication, energy, and planning. Therefore, the solutions necessitate more than simple behavior changes among individuals; they demand that "institutions of higher education need to assume a role in helping junior faculty—as well as other faculty—to accommodate the competing demands of their careers and personal lives" (Sorcinelli & Near, 1989, p. 78).

Some countries are further along the continuum toward life-friendliness than we are. Having served the world as an exemplar for decades, Sweden is well known for its progressive parental leave policies, for example. Nowadays, Swedish parents are entitled to sixteen months of leave with sixty days to be taken by the mother and sixty days by the father. The remaining 360 days are evenly split between them and can be transferred back and forth. The leave can be used full-time, half-time, quarter-time, or one-eighth-time until the child turns eight. For thirteen months parents receive 80 percent of their income and for the remaining time they receive a daily flat rate of sixty SEK per day (Klinth, 2008, p. 22).

According to research by Almqvist (2008), Swedish fathers are not merely entitled to parental leave, they also take it. She found Swedish fathers "expressed, both in practice and rhetoric, that participation in the care of children was important" (p. 198). Perhaps our research highlights a change in the zeitgeist because the younger generation of men in our study echo the same sentiment: part of how they define themselves as men is in their role as father.

The United States is not Sweden; however, a number of institutions of higher education have made great strides in assisting faculty with balancing their personal and professional lives. And they do not merely provide work-life balancing strategies the individual is free to take or leave. They go beyond and offer policies and programs that make a difference in faculty members' lives by creating the spaces and support structures necessary to engage fully in their personal and professional roles.

Although in general "academia is more focused on the business of teaching and research and not on the emerging trends in human resources," to quote an administrator interviewed for this study, exceptions exist. We chose six colleges and universities of varying sizes, locations, charters, and missions and showcased what they offer in terms of child care, spousal/partner hiring, child leave, and tenure-related policies. Some, like the University of California, Berkeley, have been at the forefront of reform for a relatively long time and are able to point to an impressive array of provisions for faculty, staff, and students. Others are smaller in scope and/or newer in the process, yet much can be learned from them as well.

Based on the study of family-friendly policies at six institutions, we will now offer recommendations and successful strategies, specifically focused on the areas of child care, spousal/partner hiring, child leave, tenure policies, communication, and change of culture. The information stems from our research on available documents, websites, and phone interviews with administrators and faculty. Special care was taken to identify those measures that are cost-neutral.

Recommendations and Successful Strategies

Tenure

Rigid tenure schedules are confining in that they do not allow the flexibility necessary to deal with major life events. Therefore, we recommend that:

- Schools and departments individually consider whether or not to lengthen the probationary period, given that a university does "not need a one-size-fits-all approach," in the words of Michigan's Provost Sullivan. This is part of a larger point: if an academic culture does not expect that all faculty do all things and do them equally well, possibilities open up for academic units to define their work as a unit, then figure out how individuals can best contribute to that work. In this way individual faculty could more easily "take turns" in getting relief for family obligations.

- Tenure extensions are granted for reasons other than childbirth, such as caring for family members or medical reasons. Doing so would address equity concerns by making all faculty, including those without new children, eligible for extensions. In addition, it would avoid the creation of "mommy tracks."

- Flexible work arrangements are introduced, as has the University of Washington, which are low-cost options with significant positive impact on work-life balancing efforts.

- Part-time options are provided for tenure-track faculty. An excellent example is the University of Washington, which allows faculty to choose among several different part-time scenarios.

- Stopping of the tenure clock in case of childbirth or adoption becomes a default option, as at the University of California, Berkeley. In case of such an event, in other words, the clock stops automatically, and faculty have to request *not* to make use of the option. As a result, tenure clock stoppage becomes the norm rather than the exception and thus loses its potentially stigmatizing character.

- Department chairs, external reviewers, and tenure and promotion committee members are made aware of the details pertaining to tenure clock stoppage to avoid the common pitfalls of the policy, namely the expectation of increased productivity when a faculty member was given "an extra year."

Spousal/Partner Hiring

Given the increasing number of dual-academic families, the issue of spousal/partner hiring, though fraught with potential dilemmas for institutions, can no longer be ignored. To make spousal/partner hiring successful, we recommend that:

- The various stakeholders work together and share the costs. Boise State serves as an example of extensive university-wide collaboration. In the case of dual hires, the chairs of those departments extending offers to primary hires, their deans, the chairs of departments that might provide employment to the spouse or partner, and the provost collaborate. For the initial three years, until a permanent line opens up, the spouse's/partner's salary, furthermore, is split three ways among the provost's office, the principal hire's department and the spouse/partner hire's department, each paying one-third.

- A central office or department, such as UCLA's Faculty Diversity and Development department, work with departments to facilitate conversations about academic career partner hiring across schools and divisions.

- Colleges and universities form or join consortiums such as the Higher Education Recruitment Consortium created by the University of Michigan or the Northern California Higher Education Resource Consortium. These organizations help find positions at nearby schools for spouses or partners who cannot be accommodated at the institution itself.

- Spouses and partners are given Web-based access not only to openings at a cluster of nearby institutions, but are also enabled to post credentials in a searchable database accessible to prospective employers.

- Ways are provided to link spouses or partners with major nonacademic employers in the area.

- Prospective hires are provided with brochures and resources so that new faculty understand that the university's commitment to dual-career couples is not simply talk but that considerable efforts are being made to help spouses and partners find gainful and appropriate employment.

- A relocation counselor is made available to help spouses or partners in conducting a fruitful job search, as is done in the University of California system.

- An office of spouse and partner employment counseling is established, as has been done at Williams College, for the purpose of career counseling and job search support to spouses and partners.

Child Leave

Pregnancy, childbirth, and adoption are major life events that increasingly affect both women's and men's careers. To ease parents' transitions into a new life phase and new responsibilities, we recommend that:

- Child leave policies are made available to both men and women not only to avoid possible disadvantages on the basis of gender and the stigmatization of women, but also to give new fathers the opportunity to care for newborns.

- Faculty are allowed to accrue sick leave that can be used for child care, as in a policy in place at Valley College.

- Faculty have flexibility in scheduling so that teaching responsibilities can be front or back loaded. For instance, Boise State allows faculty to move all teaching requirements to one semester so that it is possible to stay at home during the other semester (or leave town to care for an elder family member, for example).

- Colleges and universities offer a reduced teaching load the semester during which a new child enters the household either through birth or adoption.

- Institutions provide or create, as the UC system does, a short-term disability policy that permits four months (one semester) of child care leave.

- Universities and colleges, acknowledging the unique aspects of faculty work, provide a series of options that allow for flexibility. For instance, Williams College enables faculty to take one semester off at 3/4 pay or take a one-course reduction in teaching at full pay.

- Universities and colleges reduce the pay of faculty who go on child leave only by the amount it costs the institution to hire adjunct faculty to cover their classes.

Child Care

Child care is seen as vitally important by male and female faculty members and representatives of exemplary institutions alike, but many schools struggle with adequate provisions and long waiting lists. Even exemplary institutions may not be able to provide high-quality care to all families who desire it, including faculty, post-docs, staff, and students at both the graduate and undergraduate levels, yet successful strategies can be derived from the creativity with which they found ways to address chronic shortages. We recommend that:

- Colleges and universities create partnerships with community child-care providers, apply for small grants to give to community-based child-care providers who, in turn, allow priority access for university employees. The University of Washington serves as a model for this approach.

- Colleges and universities encourage departments to acquire grants to operate on-campus child-care facilities. For instance, the psychology department may be the appropriate place to house such a program if it offers a concentration in early childhood development. Valley College acquired grants to open a center on its campus. Thus, there are only indirect costs to the institution with grants and tuition payments covering the bulk of the expense.

- Institutions work with the state to obtain funding for child care, as exemplified by the University of Washington.

- A central office such as human resources or the provost's office creates a child-care resource program that provides a list of criteria for employees to use when looking for child care. For example, Boise State has a checklist that employees can use to assess the quality of potential child-care providers.

- Appropriate personnel or department create a babysitting coordinator who connects employees with students looking for this type of work.

- On-campus child-care facilities create flexible part-time openings that allow faculty with different schedules to utilize the high-quality child-care facilities available on campus.

- The appropriate department or office creates a resource for employees with sick children. For instance, the University of Michigan offers "Kids Kare" and UC Berkeley the "Wheezles and Sneezles" program, both of which provide a resource for employees with sick children who cannot be taken to their regular child care or school. The cost is minimal to the institution as parents carry the cost of the provider, and there are many at-home-care companies that have opened as more and more seniors wish to stay in their homes. These types of organizations would be appropriate partners for institutions looking to create a resource for employees with sick children.

Communication

Not merely having policies on the books but also communicating them well is crucial, a fact emphasized repeatedly by representatives of exemplary institutions. We recommend that:

- Because the need to communicate available policies and programs never stops, faculty, staff, administrators (especially department chairs), and students need to constantly and consistently be informed about what is available to the university community. Provost Sullivan at the University of Michigan notes that "there is an issue with educating department chairs, [and the institution] has to commit itself to a continuing education process for new hires." What makes UC Berkeley exemplary, furthermore, is the communication of policies. Professor Mary Ann Mason was one of the preparers of an in-depth guide titled "Creating a Family Friendly Department: Chairs and Deans Toolkit" (University of California, 2003b), a document detailing not only what deans and chairs ought to do, but also why. She pointed out that "the main challenge is to make sure that, at the departmental level, you have administrators and staff know what is going on. . . . Department chairs turn over every three years but the staff stays. So we have to ensure there is communication at all levels, and the staff and graduate students need to know as well." To increase awareness, Berkeley's Human Resources staff runs training sessions. According to Dr. Mason, "ultimately, everyone gets the light, but it takes a long time to do this."

- Provosts meet with every department in the process of faculty hiring to talk about policies and to encourage the department to communicate the availability of these policies and programs to applicants. These steps are meant to alleviate any fear that potential hires may have about inquiring about family-friendly policies. They do not have to bring up the topic: it is done for them.

- Information on policies and programs is provided early on in a person's career at the institution, namely along with the written acknowledgment of his or her job application package.

- At the beginning of each semester all faculty, staff, and students are sent a list of the career flexibility policies and procedures websites.

Cultural Change

Without effective communication, another characteristic of excellence is difficult to achieve, namely cultural change. "UC had progressive policies in the 80s but people were not using them," explained Dr. Mason. "Policies don't do much as long as you don't change the culture, and that never ends. It goes on for a long time." She mentioned discovering a practice at Berkeley that illustrates the profound culture change in progress. Many faculty members had discussed the problem of meetings running past 5:00 P.M., putting a strain on faculty who need to pick up children in child-care centers. Berkeley now addresses this problem head-on, and according to Dr. Mason, "we want to make sure that all faculty meetings end by 5:00." No financial cost is involved, but the institution communicates its commitment to families and their needs. Such communication, and the administration's support of family-friendly policies, may be why Dr. Mason finds that "now young faculty are taking advantage of the new policies that are in place." Similarly, it may be why faculty member Miller at UCLA believes that "Berkeley is ahead [of UCLA] in how policies are utilized because of their commitment to communicating and implementing the policies."

Some of the greatest obstacles on the road to becoming a workplace supportive of life-work balancing are deeply ingrained beliefs, often among faculty members themselves, about what it means to be a successful academic. We recommend that institutions address the following:

- The traditional notion of a linear career trajectory without acknowledgment that careers can be flexible and diverse, yet still productive.

- The perception of child leave and other policies as *accommodations* (thus potentially stigmatizing) rather than legitimate parts of a career trajectory.

- The perception that work-life balancing policies benefit only faculty with children instead of faculty in diverse family constellations, living arrangements, and at various points in their careers.

- The idea that institutions have no stake in helping faculty balance their work and family responsibilities.

In sum, a clearly discernible cultural shift away from the "ideal worker" is occurring not only inside academe but in the larger society as well, and it requires institutions of higher learning to catch up. The exemplary colleges and universities showcased here have developed an awareness of this shift and are in the process of creating and refining policies acknowledging the changing realities. Of course, their journey has not ended. "We are a work in progress but everyone is," remarked Provost Andrews at Boise State University. Even institutions with decades of experience in the work-life balancing realm are continuing to improve the packages they may be able to offer their faculty, staff and, increasingly, students. Dr. Andrews told us that she and her colleagues frequently interact with people external to Boise State with the intent of mutual learning. Although public universities are highly regulated institutions, much less nimble than many businesses and private organizations, Boise State is nevertheless often admired for its initiative in regard to work-life policies and programs.

We took a snapshot of what life-friendliness means so that other institutions might take advantage and learn from programs and policies addressing the changing needs of their faculty, regardless of gender. Certainly, the suggestion is not that colleges and universities simply adopt wholesale what exemplary institutions have done but, instead, adapt attractive policies and programs to the specific contexts of their institutions. It is our intent to disseminate successful ideas and start conversations among stakeholders about whether, to what degree, or with what kinds of modifications the programs and policies that work in progressive colleges and universities might work at theirs.

All in all, it appears that it is the combination of policies rather than one single policy that makes an institution outstanding. The ultimate goal, then, is to create a "culture of coverage," as one of our interviewees called it, meaning everyone being covered and able to meet personal challenges without having to make significant professional sacrifices. It was with that hope in mind that we wrote this book.

Appendix A

Methods

Whereas the published women's study (Philipsen, 2008) contains a quantitative element in its appendix, only qualitative parts of the women's study were considered in this book. The men's study is entirely qualitative in nature. In both cases, we were interested in faculty stories about balancing personal and professional lives because, as qualitative researcher Irving Seidman writes, "stories are a way of knowing" (Seidman, 2006, p. 7), a way for people to reflect on their experiences and give them order. According to him, when people tell stories about themselves they are making meaning about their lives by selecting details of their experience from their stream of consciousness. Seidman makes reference to Russian psychologist Lev Vygotsky, who argued that every word people use in storytelling constitutes a microcosm of their consciousness (Vygotsky, 1987, pp. 236–237). It is this consciousness that provides access to complex social and educational issues "because social and educational issues are abstractions based on the concrete experience of people" (Seidman, 2006, p. 7).

The women's study was conducted first, and after its publication (Philipsen, 2008) we decided to follow up with a parallel study including male faculty. The reasons were manifold. Though recent quantitative research on balancing issues includes the opinions of men (Mason, Goulden, & Frasch, 2009), in-depth qualitative studies on this topic are still rare. Certainly the research on men and masculinity has evolved over the last decades and no longer reflects what Chang observed sixteen years ago, namely that "men as gendered beings are usually not studied," stating further that if they are, it is from an essentialist perspective that assumes men are all the same, and their behavior is prescribed by biology (1999, p. 2). Sophisticated models of gender relations have since been developed and multiple masculinities are now recognized as constructed in specific cultural, institutional, and historical settings, all leading to more diversified views of men, masculinities, and gender relations (Connell, 2003, pp. 2–3). Yet, when it comes to our topic of how male faculty balance their personal and professional lives, research has yet to catch up, and it was our intention to help fill that void.

Participants

The women's study was based on testimony of forty-four participants while the men's study included forty-one faculty (pseudonyms used). Combined, they served seven institutions of higher education in a southeastern state, including two large, urban comprehensive public institutions, one small private liberal arts college, two HBCUs (historically black universities), a community college, and a research intensive public university (for more detail see "settings" below). Both male and female faculty were highly diverse; their disciplines including anthropology, arts, Asian studies, astrophysics, biology, business, chemistry, commerce, communications, computer science, criminal justice, culinary studies, dance, education, English, engineering, environmental studies, history, instructional technology, law, leadership studies, marketing, mathematics, medicine, music, nursing, philosophy, political science, psychology, social work, sociology, Spanish, technology, theatre, urban planning, and women's or gender studies.

The participants' age range in both studies was wide: the youngest participant was in her twenties at the time of the interview; the oldest was seventy-eight. They had worked in higher education anywhere between a few months and more than four decades. The majority possessed Ph.D.s; some had master's degrees.

The faculty members' lifestyles and personal arrangements varied. Many were married, either without children or with children living with them at home, whereas others had grown children. Living arrangements also included being single with or without children, lesbian or gay with or without partners, and "child free." Among the men, thirty-two were Caucasian, six African-American, and three immigrants from Ghana, Nigeria, and Peru. Among the women, twenty-nine were Caucasian, seven African American, and eight immigrant scholars from China, Ghana, Italy, Jamaica, Japan, the Netherlands, Pakistan, and Trinidad.

In both studies, we aimed to conduct interviews with equal numbers of faculty in three categories: early-, mid-, and late-career stages. They were defined as follows: early-career: pre-tenure, or within five years of beginning employment as a faculty member; late-career: within five years of retirement; midcareer: between early- and late-career. We realize that these markers are somewhat crude and, in addition, that career stage does not necessarily coincide with age or generational membership. We interviewed faculty members in their fifties, for instance, who served as assistant professors.

Data Collection and Analysis

The processes of data collection and analysis in the men's book mirrored those of the women's book. We used "purposeful" and "snowball" sampling, either seeking out participants via their institutional websites or relying on interviewees to recommend colleagues who might participate, always mindful to aim for equal numbers of early-, mid-, and late-career faculty and maximum diversity in terms of discipline and demographics.

IRB approval was obtained for both studies. We contacted potential participants by phone or e-mail, and the response rate was satisfactory with approximately 40–50 percent agreeing to be interviewed (the response rate for the women's book was higher at about 80 percent). The conversations in both the women's and men's studies ranged in length from fifteen minutes to an hour and a half, with most lasting for about forty-five minutes, and they were based on similar interview guides. All but two interviews were conducted in person; Maike conducted all interviews in the women's study and about half of the men's study. Tim conducted the other half for the men's study and a trained graduate assistant conducted two for the men's study.

After some small talk, we typically introduced ourselves and the project, explained the research purpose, assured participants of confidentiality, the use of pseudonyms, and the option not to answer questions, and asked for permission to tape-record. Once consent was obtained, participants provided demographic information then sketched their educational and professional histories, as well as the parameters of their personal lives (age, marital status, children, and so forth). We proceeded with a broad question asking how they saw the relationship between their professional and personal lives in general, sometimes followed by more specific probes. Open-ended questions gave participants ample opportunity to guide the conversation and talk about what was most salient to them. Included were inquiries about enabling forces and barriers to balancing their lives. We wanted to know, in other words, what factors helped them balance as well as they did, and what issues stood in their way. These questions were followed by inquiries about coping strategies they had developed and about generational differences they perceived. We also inquired about any differences the faculty members saw when they compared themselves to previous generations of faculty, and the mid- and late career participants were asked to make comparisons with newer generations of faculty. We wanted to get at their sense of history and change.

The interview concluded with questions about reform and how academic institutions ought to be changed in order to aid faculty to better balance their lives, as well as any advice they had for graduate students and faculty just beginning their careers. Although there is literature indicating that the researcher's gender matters in in-depth interviewing (Williams & Heikes, 1993), we could not discern any relevant trends in that regard. We did not find significant differences, in other words, in how the participants responded to Tim compared with how they responded to Maike.

Once data collection ceased, the interviews were transcribed verbatim and transcripts sent to all participants for member checking, inviting them to make changes (at that point, two participants in the women's study decided to withdraw). We then analyzed the data, aided by the software program ATLAS. Transcripts were coded by marking passages according to what faculty talked about (examples: barriers, enablers, coping strategies, previous generations, reform). In the men's study, a total of forty-one codes were assigned. These forty-one codes were then grouped together and, ultimately, sixteen were analyzed. One of us, for example, analyzed everything the men said about marriage, relationships, partners and children, a cluster of topics that would later form a distinct chapter. In the women's study, twenty-two codes were assigned. Once the data were coded, Maike analyzed by career stage rather than code. For example, she read everything the early career women said about "general balancing" issues or about parenting or about barriers. The end product of the women's study (Philipsen, 2008) reflects this organization.

To enhance credibility and minimize researcher bias in both studies, peer debriefing was used, meaning employing people who did not collect the data to compare raw data (interview transcripts) with interpretations derived from those data. Tim and another trained researcher (Dr. Lisa Abrams at Virginia Commonwealth University) served this function for the women's study, and for the men's study Tim and I used each other in that capacity. We both read and coded all transcripts, including those of interviews the respective other had conducted, and critically analyzed whether analyses and conclusions rang true, given what our sources had said.

The Settings

As mentioned above, we are combining in this book results of two studies (one on male and one on female faculty), and these studies took place at a total of seven institutions, none of which had progressive life-friendly policies or programs. We therefore call them "traditional institutions." In addition, we studied six colleges and universities which possess various degrees of life-friendly provisions, and we refer to these as "exemplary institutions." The following describe both types of institutions (traditional and exemplary). Pseudonyms are used for the former; real names, for the latter.

Traditional Institutions

Metropolitan University and Public Comprehensive University

Two similar universities were included in our research, both large, public, metropolitan and offering comprehensive degrees ranging from undergraduate to doctoral levels. At what we call Metropolitan University (MU), only female faculty were interviewed. MU prides itself on being the largest university in the state, serving more than 30,000 students. Its buildings and facilities are scattered throughout a major southern city, space and expansion being a challenge. MU aspires to improve its research status and rise from "research intensive" to "research extensive" according to the most recent Carnegie categorization scheme. Faculty members tend to have relatively heavy teaching loads and students are diverse in background, frequently first-generation college-going and often part-time. Many need a lot of support to succeed academically.

The other university of this type, Public Comprehensive University, is located in a different part of the state and serves approximately 21,000 students. We interviewed only male faculty there. Its facilities are located about three miles from the downtown area of a major southern city, and though the buildings are spread out, there has been a concerted effort to create a more geographically defined "campus." This effort has occurred in conjunction with a rapid expansion in enrollment and research activity in the last ten years. Public Comprehensive University is classified as a Carnegie Research Institution with a "high" research activity. Teaching loads are heavy as well, and the student body resembles that of Metropolitan University: diverse in background, a high proportion of first-generation college-going and part-time, often in need of intense academic support.

Flagship University

We interviewed both male and female faculty at Flagship. It is a selective public research institution serving about 20,000 students in a pristine setting, a small university town surrounded by wooded hills. Faculty members typically emphasize research more than teaching and service, and students have the reputation of being strong academically.

Private Comprehensive

Both male and female faculty were interviewed at Private Comprehensive which enrolls about 4,500 students attracted from a wide geographic area. Its beautiful campus, located in an upscale residential district of a large city, and high rankings in magazine surveys have helped make it relatively selective in recent years. It offers both undergraduate and graduate professional degrees.

Community College

Faculty of both genders were interviewed at Community College. Community College serves 17,000 students on three campuses in a metropolitan area, preparing students for transfer to four-year college institutions, employment, and more. Although the emphasis on scholarly activity of the faculty has increased somewhat, teaching is by far where faculty spend most of their time.

HBCU One and HBCU Two

Both HBCUs are located in midsize towns, one serving almost 5,000, the other almost 7,000 students. Only female faculty were interviewed at HBCU ONE and only male faculty at HBCU TWO. Due to their relatively open enrollment policy, they attract students with varying degrees of academic preparation, many of whom need a lot of faculty attention. Teaching loads are high and the emphasis on research is relatively low compared with other institutions of higher education.

Exemplary Institutions

Once we had completed the men's study, and realized that many of the younger generations of male faculty began to experience challenges similar to those of their female colleagues, we became curious to learn what institutions throughout the United States were doing that might more effectively address the needs the faculty in our research had expressed. How can the change that both men and women demand be accomplished?

We decided to showcase selected schools that distinguish themselves through the exemplary packages they make available to faculty, often staff and, to some extent, students. By doing so, we are hoping to provide assistance to colleges and universities that are striving to make their campuses more conducive to the realities that faculty face. In many instances, the initiatives of these exemplary institutions are not economically prohibitive, another appealing feature for anyone seeking to replicate their efforts. Further, even if there are costs involved, it is crucial to weigh those against the costs of faculty leaving for more progressive institutions or hampering faculty success because they are unable to manage the demands at both home and work.

In order to decide which institutions might qualify as "exemplary," we pursued a number of avenues. For one, we asked experts in the field for top-ranked places. Secondly, we searched the literature and, thirdly, we visited websites looking for exemplary policies and programs. As mentioned previously, we sought to diversify and include not merely top-ranked and well-endowed schools but those that varied in location, size, charter, mission, student profile, and budget size. Doing so meant that, in some instances, policies and programs cannot be considered "top-of the line" but are works in progress. We include them in this book because they are illustrative of what a variety of institutions might be able to do on the road to life-friendliness.

It was easy to find the leading institutions in the realm of life-friendly policies, and we selected among them the research-intensive, internationally known, and relatively well-funded public universities of UC Berkeley and UCLA, Michigan, and Washington. Selective, private, liberal-arts colleges like Williams College that had impressive life-friendly packages were easy to identify as well. The search for community colleges, public comprehensives, or HBCUs was more complex, but we succeeded nevertheless. The ultimate challenge, after all, is not only to discern and describe what works in making an institution life-friendly, but also to find out ways in which diverse schools are able to implement the ideas.

Once we decided whom to include in the study, we sent e-mail invitations to administrators and faculty instrumental in designing or implementing life-friendly policies, and asked for phone interviews. Those were granted in almost all cases. Consequently, we talked to the informants for about thirty to forty-five minutes, particularly about the history of the policies at their institution, their flaws, challenges, and those aspects not readily discernible from the outside.

Once we wrote up the policies and programs at a given college or university, we sent drafts to the interviewees for member checking and feedback. They were asked to check for accuracy, make any changes they wished, and indicate whether they wanted us to use their real names or pseudonyms instead. Their responses proved invaluable in that they enriched our document analysis, gave it more depth, and provided experience-based information for those who hope to replicate their work.

The following is a brief overview of the exemplary institutions showcased in this study.

University of Washington

Note: unless otherwise indicated, all information for the University of Washington (UW) is derived from the University of Washington's websites and their links:

www.washington.edu/

www.washington.edu/admin/acadpers/index.html

www.washington.edu/provost/initiatives/balance/

UW was founded in 1861, which makes it one of the oldest state-supported institutions of higher education on the West Coast. With an enrollment of over 40,000 students and an endowment of $1.6 billion, the university is internationally known for the high quality of its research and graduate programs.

The following message can be found on the Academic Human Resources homepage: "The UW has a comprehensive package of policies and programs designed to support faculty in balancing productive academic careers with satisfying personal lives. Our goal is to support faculty through the various stages of life. This will enhance the ability of UW to recruit and retain the best and brightest faculty, and enhance the ability of faculty to perform their best teaching and research" (University of Washington, n.d.-a).

According to Quinn and Shapiro (2009), the University of Washington has a thirty-year history of supporting the work-family relationship of its faculty, staff and students. Groups representing these three constituencies worked with the offices of WorkLife and the vice provost for Academic Personnel to enact family-friendly policies and programs, and they have resulted in numerous life-friendly awards and grants, including the 2001 ADVANCE institutional transformation grant awarded by the National Science Foundation. Incoming president Mark Emmert launched the Leadership, Community and Values Initiative in 2005, leading to a further enhancement in the institution's commitment to supporting work-life balancing (Quinn & Shapiro, 2009).

University of Michigan

Note: unless otherwise indicated, all information about the University of Michigan is derived from the University of Michigan's websites and their links:

www.umich.edu/

www.hr.umich.edu/childcare/index.html

www.hr.umich.edu/worklife/index.php

www.provost.umich.edu/faculty/family/index.html

The University of Michigan was founded in 1817 in Detroit. It was not until 1837 that Ann Arbor became its official home (University of Michigan, 2010). Today UM serves over 40,000 students from all fifty states and 117 countries. According to Jeff Frumkin, assistant provost and senior director of Academic Human Resources, UM's concern with work-life balance issues "goes back to the early 90s." Its commitment to assisting faculty in balancing their work-life responsibilities is evident in what the president believes is part of the University's mission. The president is quoted as proclaiming that "supporting our faculty as they balance their professional and personal lives is a high priority" (University of Michigan, 2005b). This attitude is echoed by Provost Sullivan who told us that the University of Michigan "wants to be an employer of choice." In order to clarify the extent of this commit-ment to work-life balance issues, we will discuss the provisions the institution makes for child care, spousal/partner hiring, new child leave, and in its tenure policies.

University of California

Note: unless otherwise indicated, all information about the University of California (UC) is derived from the University of California, Berkeley's and Los Angeles's websites and their links:

http://workandfamily.chance.berkeley.edu/

http://berkeley.edu/

www.ucla.edu/

www.faculty.diversity.ucla.edu/worklife/index.htm

As a system, the University of California offers some of the best work-life policies and benefits available in U.S. institutions of higher education. The Berkeley campus opened in 1869 in Oakland and moved to its present location in 1873. The institu-tion was a merger of a private college in Oakland and a new land grant institution, and it serves 35,409 graduate and undergraduate students today.

Founded in 1919 as the southern branch of the University of California and presenting programs to 260 junior college stu-dents and 1,078 students in its teacher training program, the Los Angeles campus today has a total student enrollment of 37,476 undergraduate and graduate students. The University of California's mission "is to serve society as a center of higher learning, providing long-term societal benefits through transmitting advanced knowledge, discovering new knowledge, and functioning as an active working repository of organized knowledge" (University of California, 2004).

The policies offered by the University of California (UC) are, as Mary Ann Mason, professor and codirector of the Center for Economics & Family Security at the University of California, Berkeley's School of Law, put it, "the floor but not the ceiling." Each campus can add to the system's package. Considering that these "floor" policies represent an understanding of the importance of work-life issues for faculty that goes well beyond any of the institutions included in our interview study, it would seem that more colleges and universities would strive to match, at the very least, these policies in order to attract and retain the best possible faculty and graduate students.

Williams College

Note: unless otherwise indicated, all information about Williams is derived from the following Williams College websites and their links:

www.williams.edu

www.williams.edu/admin/vp_diversity/

Though not as large as the other institutions we have highlighted as exemplary, Williams College, a private liberal arts institution, strives to create policies and programs to assist faculty with balancing work-life responsibilities on a scale commensurate with its size. It may, therefore, well serve as an example for other, similarly sized colleges. Established in 1793, Williams has a total student enrollment of 2,185 students with 33 majors as well as concentrations and special programs (Williams College, 2010a). Williams' mission is to "provide the finest possible liberal arts education by nurturing in students the academic and civic virtues, and their related characteristics" (Williams College, 2010b).

Boise State University

Note: Unless otherwise indicated the information about Boise State is derived from the following websites and their links:

www.boisestate.edu/future

www.boisestate.edu/deptchairs/career.shtml

Boise State University is a metropolitan research university, located in Idaho's capital. Consisting of seven colleges, its undergraduate and graduate programs serve almost 20,000 students in more than 190 fields of interest (Boise State University, n.d.-b). Though its formal efforts at becoming life-friendly began only a few years ago, the university has made remarkable strides in designing and implementing progressive policies and programs to serve its faculty, staff, and students.

San Bernardino Valley College

Note: unless otherwise indicated, all information about Valley College is derived from the following websites and their links:

www.valleycollege.edu/

www.sbccd.org/pages/1.asp

To diversify the sample of exemplary institutions, we sought to include a community college and, though its life-friendly provisions pale in comparison with those offered at the other institutions showcased, Valley College did have some notable programs and policies in place that assist its faculty with work-life balancing.

The history and organization of the community college system in California is unique. The San Bernardino Community College District (SBCCD) is one of seventy-two community college districts in California with a mission "to promote the discovery and application of knowledge, the acquisition of skills, and the development of intellect and character in a manner that prepares students to contribute effectively and ethically as citizens of a rapidly changing and increasingly technological world" (SBCCD, 2010b). Each district then contains a certain number of colleges and centers located within its boundaries, and San Bernardino Valley College (Valley College) is one of the campuses in SBCC.

Appendix B

Additional Findings from the Men's Study

Finding Words to Describe It

Certainly as an academic, and particularly as a post-tenured academic, I have enormous freedom in how I live my life.

Consistent with prior research on academic women (Philipsen, 2008), male faculty members' ideals of what constitutes a happy balance between the personal and professional vary significantly. Quite a number of men strive to merge the different spheres of their lives while others seek to keep them separate. Some always take work home and live a blended existence, and one person even reports total overlap given that he essentially chooses not to have a personal life at all. Others do not mix the two but draw a clear line, leaving their work at the office and going home to assume various roles.

Being relatively autonomous in deciding the relationship between personal and professional spheres of life is a privilege not many professions award their members. Colbeck (2006, p. 36) noted that, compared, for instance, with shift work, academic work allows for a higher degree of choice in how flexible and permeable the boundaries between work and life are to be. Though research on female faculty (Philipsen, 2008) has shown that this freedom of choice is largely confined to late-career women, in the case of the men in this study, career stage does not seem to make a difference. Instead, men determine the work-life relationship regardless of whether they are of junior or senior status.

When asked how they view the relationship between their personal and professional lives, most men, including those at the junior level, sound positive, a remarkable fact given that the earliest years in a faculty member's career life cycle are likely to be the most difficult ones (Olsen & Sorcinelli, 1992), and for women, balancing acts between the personal and professional contribute to these difficulties (Philipsen, 2008). In fact, Philipsen (2008) describes how early- and midcareer women report great strains trying to establish and maintain a healthy balance between their personal and professional lives, and only late-career women have reached relative contentment. At first glance, the men in this study, regardless of generation, paint a different picture, all sounding fairly positive about their work-life relationships. This study's findings, in conjunction with those of the previous study on female faculty, are consistent with earlier research showing that whereas levels of work-family conflict were only moderately lower in each consecutive life-cycle stage for men, levels of conflict for women dropped significantly in later life-cycle stages (Higgins, Duxbury, & Lee, 1994).

And yet the male faculty members' positive accounts should not distract from the fact that the younger-generation men are beginning to encounter significant challenges to their work-life balances. This apparent discrepancy suggests that a closer look at the astonishingly positive testimony of academic men across career stages is warranted.

"I'm very pleased with the balance," says Assistant Professor Johnson, "we have a lot of freedom to structure our time, and that's been nice." In comparison with his former professional life as a nurse, another early-career professor points out that he is now able to protect his private sphere much more than in the past when patients called him at all hours. A colleague, also at the pre-tenure level, says he can now go to the grocery store in the middle of the day, something he was unable to do when he worked in industry before entering academe. Much of his work is done at home because he does not have to punch a time clock. Though he works a lot, he says, he does not mind because it is work he enjoys. "I'm very happy!" he insists. "The job that I have really allows me to pursue the things that I want to outside of academia." He calls himself a workaholic and freely admits that he takes care of work first, often avoiding visits to his mother and father. "I always find excuses not to be with them."

Another junior faculty member compares himself with his wife and concludes he works less than she does in her role as a schoolteacher. He also compares his current life as a faculty member at a small liberal arts college with his Ph.D. program in organic chemistry at an elite university. He finds his workload much more doable, and thus his balance significantly healthier. "When we were in graduate school," he remembers, "a sixty hour work week would have been considered a minimum."

Mid- and late-career faculty sound similarly positive, and though they may not view the relationship as ideal, most do not voice strong complaints, either. The personal and professional lives "work pretty well together," according to Professor Jankovitch, and "it's been working for thirty-three years now." Along similar lines, late-career Professor Ingrahm feels that he is in a better balance now than he used to be when he got too involved in his research and work separated him from his family, who felt shut out. "But I think that's evened out now," he says. "I've got a good relationship with all three members of my family."

Dr. Dotolo at Private Comprehensive has reached a relatively healthy balance as well, despite the fact that "sometimes the work backs up and bumps too much into the home, and that's not a good thing." "They're just two sides of the same coin," is how Professor Jarman characterizes the relationship between his personal and professional life. "I don't really think of it in any special way. I do my job; I go home and have a family life. That's about all." Dr. Metzger at Flagship recently retired but stays active in many professional roles and, looking back at his long career, feels that he was able to craft a very close relationship between his personal and professional lives. "I think that what happens is when you can't distinguish them, maybe that's the place where it has most satisfaction associated with it." He describes how he never thought about balancing different parts of his life; to him, the professional and the personal were the same. He grew up in a blue-collar family and in that culture, he says, work was one thing, and your life was something else. More precisely, work was something you had to do, and your life was something you chose to do. In his case, however, things were different and it became clear to him that "what you did at work and what you did personally just because you loved it, could be the same thing."

Dr. Lewis at Public Comprehensive also expresses satisfaction with his life: "I am very happy with the balance I have achieved at this point," he exclaims, echoed by others:

- "I don't find any kind of conflict there. I guess I could say they [the professional life and life outside of the academy] work together very nicely in that I do have a good bit of latitude as to when I do my work, so therefore also when I do my play, and I like that balance."

- "I don't think there was ever . . . any problem."

- "Now is a wonderful balance between professional and personal life."

- "I would categorize myself as the happiest time of my life with regards to those things. . . . Basically, all in the balance, I am very happy with how things are going."

To reiterate, it is remarkable that not just senior faculty who are tenured, or have otherwise distinguished themselves, paint the relationships between the personal and professional as an easy

one, but that their junior colleagues do it as well. A look at some
of the testimony given in the comparable study on women makes
the contrast especially stark. The following are typical statements
characterizing the early- and midcareer faculty (all quotes taken
from Philipsen, 2008).

- "Am I able to balance. . . ? I would say 'no.' Not at all."
- "I have to learn that since you make the optional choice
  to work, you have to give up something. With a family,
  you can't do both equally. One will have to give."
- "I think women, more than anything else, struggle. . . .
  Men for the most part, I don't see that as a big struggle
  for most men. Work as hard as necessary to attain that
  goal for my job, and struggle over how much time I give
  my family, or how much quality time. . . . I see that is
  something that women, because we are nurturers and
  because culturally, we see our role as being available,
  that we struggle with it."
- "There is no balance. It is only work, work, work."
- "Many women have a lot of balls in the air and feel
  stretched way thin."

It would be premature to conclude, after reading the starkly
different testimony between genders, that men simply have easier
lives than women. As will become obvious in subsequent chapters, especially early-career and, to some degree, midcareer men,
are increasingly struggling with challenges similar to those faced
by their female colleagues. Why they nevertheless portray their
overall balancing acts so positively is not entirely clear. What
could be at play is what survey researchers call "social desirabil-
ity bias," meaning a tendency, especially in face-to-face situations, to give answers through a filter of what makes people look
good (Babbie, 1983). This explanation would help account for

the differences between the generally positive tone of the male faculty in this study, not just in regard to their balancing acts but their careers generally, and the results of large survey research that shows academic job satisfaction having eroded significantly over the past generation (Schuster & Finkelstein, 2006, pp. 148–156). So perhaps the men would respond differently on surveys than they did in face-to-face situations. The question remains, however, why this phenomenon did not occur during the women's study (Philipsen, 2008).

Perhaps a gender-based explanation bears more fruit here, one that addresses the desire among the male participants to avoid coming across as whiners and complainers. It might be perceived as culturally appropriate for women to voice work-life challenges but not for men. Could this have to do with many men's deeply ingrained need to be in control, and the fear that admitting their life balance to be out of whack might be interpreted as an indication of an inability to control all parts of their lives or how they relate to each other? Michael Schwalbe and Michelle Wolkomir discuss how the masculine self influences the interview situation. They write that in Western culture, the definition of manhood requires men to distinguish themselves from women, and they do so, among other things, by trying to be more autonomous in thought and action, more rational, and better able to control people and the world (Schwalbe & Wolkomir, 2003, p. 56).

"From the moment of his birth until the moment of his death, a male is caught up in three different dimensions of control," writes Eli Newberger in his book on the nature and nurture of the male character (1999, p. 160). These three forms, according to him, encompass the control of the environment, containing the environment's efforts to control the male, and self-control. A man who has been successful in the process of establishing all three forms of control, then, will have a sufficient degree of influence within his environment to live a satisfying life, will be powerful enough to prevent being exploited, and will be able to respond thoughtfully to challenges (Newberger, 1999, p. 163). Put in these terms, admitting that one has not been able to sufficiently control one's environment and, instead, has seen it spin out of balance, thus out of control, reeks of individual failure and goes against what might be considered male nature. Instead, the male faculty member says: "My life-work balance is fine, thank you very much."

It is further noteworthy that the men in this study tend to think about their balancing acts in comparative terms. They compare the amount of available free time to what they faced in competitive graduate and post-doc programs, or to the free time of previous generations, and they appreciate the relative gains. They draw comparisons with blue-collar workers and conclude that they do not fare so badly, or with people working in other professions and at other institutions. Whereas the women typically speak about their balancing acts in absolute terms, the men put things in perspective and conclude that, all things considered, they are able to balance fairly well. More research is needed, however, to help tease out how to account for these differences.

The relatively positive tone of the men's discourse about life-work balancing should not distract from the challenges that lurk below the surface. Costs and sacrifice resulting from difficult work-life situations are addressed in the next section.

Challenge and Sacrifice

So a whole bunch of people . . . they're paying a tremendous family price to be gone all the time.

The academic career, and the preparation for it, is often consuming, if not insatiable, in its demands on time and attention. As 61-year-old Professor Rabinowitz sums it up: "There were times in my career when I simply gave up a personal life. . . . There were simply sacrifices that had to be made."

Pursuing such an all-consuming career, then, likely affects personal relationships, and so it is no surprise that the men in this study have lost relationships, or come close to it, because of extreme career demands. Midcareer Professor Ashcroft remembers how he and his wife began to drift apart because their geographical life centers were in different places given that he was traveling frequently in addition to working in a city far away from their residence. At some point he remembers saying, "I think I left my wife."

Assistant Professor Williams at Private Comprehensive knows about leaving. He is 32 years old and married for the second time. His first wife wondered, he says, whether he was married to her or to Harvard University given the excessive amount he had to work pursuing his Ph.D. and post-doc. Dr. Mahoney's first marriage also broke up in graduate school, and the fact that "there is only so much time" was a contributing factor. He tries to be more mindful in his second relationship but knows that here, too, he has missed out on things with his partner and the larger family because of work, primarily travel. "Travel is one of those non-compressible things," he says and quotes Woody Allen as saying "ninety percent of life is just showing up." You really have to be at the right events, he explains, show the flag, and establish the personal connections which then, in turn, translate into invitations to serve on committees and review boards. Being at events is vital, especially when you are trying to establish yourself, but "that's time away from your family." He remembers canceling his participation in a cruise his partner's family had organized and paid for, purchasing nonrefundable tickets no less, because an invitation to speak at a workshop in London came up. "So not only was it a week with her family, and the extended family; family is very important to her. . . . And I was good, but that's a trip you make by yourself. And in this case, everyone else was literally off in the sun and fun, and those are the kinds of tradeoffs that you make. . . . And so the conferences, the need to attend so many of them, do tend to be an obstacle."

Sixty-six-year-old Professor Green's opinion is that divorces are extremely common in académe: "All my close friends have been married at least twice," he says. "It's just an occupational hazard. It happens all the time." His first marriage broke up because of how he handled career demands. "I was focused on going back to school, and it was at the expense of my family," he recounts. The increase in the divorce rate of Dr. Green's generation was not confined to academics, of course. Researcher Arlie Hochschild described back in 1989 how over the last several decades, an increasing number of American women had begun to work outside the home, and the divorce rate had increased. She interpreted the finding differently from some of her contemporaries who claimed that women's work caused divorce; she argues instead that a decisive factor lies in whether or not husbands did a sizable share of the domestic work (Hochschild, 1989/2001).

Dr. Selinski initially did not choose his career over his marriage but vice versa, and this conflict over profession and family caused him to be unemployed for four years. His marriage finally fell apart, after all. He had applied for and was offered the job at a small university in Texas, he remembers, but his wife refused to move. This is the story.

> It looked like a job that was perfect for me. So I was very happy. And my wife refused to go. She said, "You've got a choice. You can take me, or you can take the job." And, in fact, the department chairman called me one morning to find out what my decision was, and my wife and I had just been having a very heated discussion over this, so here I was with him on one end of the line and her standing right next to me, and . . . I finally . . . said, "I'm going to have to decline the offer." That was really a mistake in retrospect because I was doing it to try and save my marriage, and, frankly, there was no way to save that marriage. So then I spent four years unemployed. I was

working shoveling driveways in the winter, pruning fruit
trees, building gardens, painting houses, doing construction on houses as need be, and I was working sixteen,
eighteen, twenty hours a day, six days a week, just to
survive. And finally I managed to put things together,
and I got a job offer in Brazil, and my wife said the same
thing, "You've got a choice between me and the job,"
and at this point I realized that that was pointless, and
I said, "I'm going to Brazil."

Late-career Professor Jackson at Flagship University has his
own regrets surrounding professional sacrifices he made for the
sake of his family. He took a tenure-track position at Flagship
rather than stay at his previous, highly prestigious institution,
which had not offered him tenure. "There were a number of decisions made in my life that were made because of family," he says.
"This job was an offer you don't refuse if you have 'hostages of for-
tune,' Sir Francis Bacon's phrase for a man's wife and children."

While Senior Professor Zavella exclaims that he is "at a station
in life that's fantastic. I'm an empty nester," he also emphasizes that
he had to make a conscious effort at reaching this happy state and
setting priorities. Doing so involved professional sacrifices. To him,
family comes first, and when he was asked why he is not publishing
in certain journals or not maximizing his potential, he responded
that the personal goals of others may not apply to him. Dr. Ashcroft
at HBCU echoes these sentiments. "I'm not doing it anymore," he
emphasizes, meaning that he is no longer spending extraordinary
amounts of time on his work. Instead, he weighs carefully what
is important in life, and chooses accordingly. Dr. Sneed at Public
Comprehensive also made a decision that "it really wasn't worth it."
He recalls being "obsessed with work to the detriment of the family"
as a graduate student and junior faculty member, which "had the
result of pretty much screwing up my family life forever." He had
heart surgery, and "something happened, and I don't remember

if it was the heart surgery, but I remember sitting down and thinking I can be the best professor in the world at what I do, or I can try to be a good husband and father, and be a really good professor. And so instead of staying out all night and working . . . I decided that it really wasn't worth it. . . . So there is a nice balance at this point. I think there has been for a pretty good while."

Dr. Dennison, full professor and department chair at Flagship, is less sanguine about his balancing act; in fact, he has reached the conclusion that his family is "not coping." For a time, he commuted from his place of employment on the east coast to the Midwest where his wife had a faculty appointment. When the strain became too great, she found a position on the east coast, but it is a four-hour commute from his institution. He knows that the "set of conflicts that we clearly resolved in one way [were not resolved] without consequences." It caused his wife to get "quite depressed about where her professional life has taken her," and the compromise has left both feeling either professionally or personally frustrated. Because his wife's appointment is in a city so far away, she now stays gone for part of the week, rendering Dr. Dennison the single father of their five-year old twins. Although not all commuter relationships are as difficult as Dr. Dennison's (Bloom, 2005), he feels tremendously stressed and, in his own words, "vulnerable." His marriage is slipping, and it has much to do with the extreme strains the commuter- and dual-career couple faces. In order to get everything done, Dr. Dennison gets up at 4:00 A.M. which means that he also goes to bed right after he puts his children down. "That means I do absolutely nothing at night," he says. "That's a coping strategy, it also has painful consequences." His wife does not share his schedule, and so "we're sort of crossing paths. Times for intimacy and times for exchanging information and thoughts and stuff are harder to come by because of my schedule. So it's coping in one sense, but the opposite in another."

It is not just the relationship with his wife that bears the costs often associated with two academics trying to pursue their careers;

it is also his relationship with his children. Remembering his commute during the first year of their lives, Dr. Dennison states: "Clearly, I never imagined putting myself in a personal position where I . . . wouldn't see my children for five days. The first year of their lives I commuted from here to Kansas, and so I would fly home every weekend but my wife had the kids during the week. And I never could have imagined doing that, it would have seemed crazy, and very inconsistent with what I wanted out of a family. . . . It was my impetus to have these kids, what was I doing spending eighty percent of my time away from the kids?" Sometimes he wonders: "What would my professional life be if I had the kind of home life that somebody ten years older than me had?" Ten-year-old research indicates that, at the time, young children in the household produced significantly negative impacts on success in balancing paid work and family life, but only for full-time employed women, not for fully employed men (Milkie & Peltola, 1999, p. 488), a finding that appears questionable today.

Indeed, Dr. Dennison emphasizes that men's experiences of work and home are much more similar to women's experiences of work and home today than they were in his father's generation, or than they were even ten years ago. Women, for one, feel less often that they have to choose between having children and having a career, whereas men cannot simply launch into a career expecting that they will spend however much time it takes them to do their career while their wives take care of the children. Dual-career families, however, complicate lives.

The changing times and the increased involvement in domestic affairs and parenting are not always easy, as Assistant Professor Trenton would agree. It is good that it is more acceptable now for male faculty to spend more time with their families; however, if one needs child care, and the wife's salary is low, dual-earner existence brings with it financial problems. In addition, on a day-to-day basis "it's a big coordination problem."

Today's men, just as their families, simply have more to worry about than previous generations, and life may have been simpler "back then" is the consensus. Alex Landers at Community College quotes a member of his church saying that "people today are running around doing a lot of good things, but not doing . . . what's best for the family." They do soccer, clarinet practice, the YMCA, but that may not be the best way to spend time. They don't take time to have dinner together, see what the kids are watching on TV. And that is something unique to the younger generation, he thinks, and was not as prevalent in the past. "I don't think that generations before had to worry about running here, running there . . . and all that," he concludes. Society places value on these activities, in his opinion, and he knows people who feel they are not good parents unless they are involved in clubs and activities with their kids. He describes a lifestyle of parents similarly to how author Judith Warner described "motherhood in the age of anxiety," namely as "perfect madness" (Warner, 2005). When Mr. Landers grew up, in comparison, he recounts: "I wasn't in much but I felt like I was in a good home."

Although "mad parenting" may largely be a self-made problem, engaged parenting is often difficult for academics. Professor emerita at San Diego State University Kathleen B. Jones writes that "'[m]othering' and academia still don't belong together" (Jones, 2005, p. 181); neither, we assert, do "fathering" and academia or, to put it differently "[u]niversity policy and academic culture continue to discourage men from being active parents" (Mason, 2009). Early-career male faculty make their marriage and children a priority, and many of them purposely chose a career in academe in order to have time to be a good husband and father. Yet having children produces challenges and demands sacrifices. "With small kids it's hard," says Assistant Professor Allison, whose wife works in the same department as he does. "Their schedules don't always match up well with our schedules. Like today, for example, I have a meeting . . . and Elise and I both need to be there. This is one of those instances where we're not able to work it out between the two of us. . . . We're going to have to end up doing this, and our daughter is going to have to get into one of our offices coloring while we're meeting down the hall here." Often he feels pulled between what he needs to get done at home and at work, and that can be frustrating. "There are so many times when you feel like you're just putting out fires," he says. He likes to have blocks of uninterrupted time to work, and those are hard to come by at home. "So yeah, you definitely feel that frustration between trying to separate the two [spheres]."

Given the equal nature of their marriages and partnerships, many male faculty find themselves called upon to handle crises with their children, something that in the past would have been the sole responsibility of the mother. Early-career faculty member at HBCU Professor Ampofo, who commutes 75 miles home, remembers his panic when he received a call from his child's day care. He was told that his son ran a 103-degree fever, and his wife could not be reached. The child needed to be taken to the hospital, and there was no parent available. While driving 90 miles an hour to get there as soon as possible, he continuously attempted to contact his wife. Finally, he reached her; she had had her phone off because she was in a meeting. At this point, they decided to meet at the hospital, and everything worked out fine, eventually.

Professor Ionesco at the same institution points out that because he had more flexibility in his work schedule than his wife, it was he who had to juggle to take care of his children when they were ill. He notes that he would say to his department head: "I really need to go because one of my kids is sick. So I'd have to ask a colleague to cover my classes; I don't care; I have to go." The possibility of negative repercussions did not concern him given that he had made a commitment to be there for his children.

Motherhood and guilt have long been closely associated and have provided rich fodder for analysis. Tarshia Stanley at Spelman College, for instance, claims that motherhood and guilt ("mother-guilt") go hand in hand, and academe takes this guilt to new levels beyond what is customary in other realms of society (Stanley, 2005). Younger male faculty in this study serve as reminders that "fatherguilt" may well be a growing phenomenon leaving men in the academy feeling just as torn and inadequate to master the challenges of professional and personal lives as used to be true primarily for their female colleagues. Increasingly they, just like women, are operating in a system of "domesticity," defined by Joan Williams as a gender system built on the ideal of a full-time worker who takes little or no time off for childbearing or rearing. Though the ideal-worker norm may not define all jobs, it does define the "good" ones such as those of the professional middle class. In this system, her argument continues, caregivers tend to be unable to perform as ideal workers and are often marginalized (Williams, 2000, p. 1). To reiterate, our study shows that this marginalization is no longer exclusively a women's issue. It follows then that "[i]f we as a society take seriously children's needs for parental care, it is time to stop marginalizing the adults who provide it" (Williams, 2000, p. 63), and these adults more and more often consist of both women and men.

To cope with the challenges just described, younger generations of male faculty are beginning to adopt a strategy they call "hyper-planning." Though an effective coping mechanism, it bears its own costs and diminishes the quality of people's lives. Hyper-planning simply means that, in order to coordinate the schedules of two working parents and to ensure that nothing is forgotten, faculty members plan and account for almost all of their time.

Professor Molina of Community College says he and his wife handle their demanding lives by "just working out schedules and doing what we call business meetings where we go, I pull out my day book, and she pulls out her Lotus Notes, and we just go day by day for the next month and nail things down." This process ensures that they each know what the other one is doing and that they cover for each other picking up their children from day care and taking care of them. Finding themselves in what has been called a "half-changed world" (Orenstein, 2000, quoted in Gornick & Meyers, 2005, p. 373), some men in the study plan every moment of their day in order to stay on track and to accomplish what is required of them, struggling with work-family conflicts hardly known even a single generation ago (Gornick & Meyers, 2005, p. 373). Dr. McDaniels, a midcareer professor at Community College, says:

> We're up at 5:30; we're getting the kids up and trying to get them fed and get everybody to the bus stop, and then I maybe find five or ten minutes to try to read the paper before I come into work and grab me something to eat. . . . [My wife] gets off at 5:00 and picks the kids up from [their] after school [program]. . . . It's tough sometimes because we're also involved in things with church, in the evening during the week, so it's a matter of trying to pick them up and get home and get something to eat, and then maybe we're off to choir rehearsal or we're off to some meeting or something at church. I'm also active in a couple of civic organizations, so we just try to balance all of that.

This type of schedule seems typical. Professor Ampofo at HBCU elucidates this process in discussing what happens when his wife, also an academic, has to leave town:

> I'll finish my classes and do all the things I need to do, and I do a little, if I can, with my research, and then let's say like around 4 PM I'll start racing back to home. I'll pick up the older kid, and then I'll pick up the younger kid from day care and then I'll take them home, wash them, feed them. . . . So my logic is let's say around

8 o'clock I'll be done with the kids. I give them all the
attention they need. I help them with their homework
and play with them, and then by 8 o'clock I should have
them in bed. Then I can make it back to my work.

Professor Allison at Public Comprehensive and his wife utilize
an electronic scheduling system to keep themselves on track. He
says, "We kind of both have our own calendar on Yahoo or whatever, and we're both able to look at each other's, and she'll send
me appointments and stuff so that I'll know about it." The ingenuity exhibited to keep everything going proves admirable; it is
disconcerting, however, that hyper-planning describes the reality
of a growing number of families.

Although members of the younger generations use hyper-
planning as well as other strategies to manage their lives, some
older faculty made different choices that proved to have their
own downsides. Not having been able to spend more time with
his children growing up and his ailing parents before they died, for
instance, is one of the major regrets of late-career faculty Thompson
at Community College. He is sorry for not having found the time to
make his family more of a priority. Late-career Professor Green at
Private Comprehensive remembers that when the family was young,
his personal and professional lives were not compatible, extract-
ing a high price. "We had some difficulties," he says and describes
problems in his first marriage when the children were growing up,
and he was working full-time in addition to obtaining an advanced
degree. He concedes that though both he and his wife worked outside of the home, he had "these traditional notions and I was, I sup-
pose, the typical male at that time. She would work all day, just like
I would, but then she would come home and take care of the meals
and take care of the children. And it wasn't fair but I wasn't sensitive to those issues at the time, and of course this led to problems."

Whereas some faculty members' relationships suffer as a consequence of their career choices, others are not able to establish

any lasting relationships in the first place, as in the case of Private Comprehensive's Associate Professor Price. When asked about the balancing between his personal and professional lives he responds: "I start out with a joke. What personal life?" Being out of town and out of the country for extended periods of time made it difficult for him to be in a committed relationship, and he now finds himself a single man at age 46 who has never been married. He calls his second-guessing of life choices "the natural result of somebody now sliding quickly toward fifty and running out of friends who are single," and muses: "There is something that I will never have . . . like somebody you're going home to." People who are in serious relationships, he thinks, do not have to make time for a personal life; it is already there in the form of a person to whom one has made a lifetime commitment.

As previously mentioned, single men in academe are relative rarities. According to Dr. Price he is the only single man not only in his department but also in two related disciplines at his college, and his observation is consistent with national statistics. According to previous research, tenured women in science are twice as likely as tenured men to be single, and more tenured women remain single in the social sciences and humanities (Mason & Goulden, 2002). Yet and still, single faculty men exist, and their bachelorhoods may not be entirely voluntary but a cost associated with career demands not conducive to finding and building lasting relationships.

The challenges of the faculty career do not just jeopardize relationships but, in some instances, the faculty member's health. It took Assistant Professor Daughtrey at Private Comprehensive, for example, 14 years after he was granted his degree to find a tenure-track position. His wife is an academic, too, and the couple vowed never to live separately. The extreme job insecurities in the past, however, took their toll on Dr. Daughtrey's health. "I was having terrible insomnia problems," he recalls. "I never felt comfortable, I never felt like things were secure. And the result of it was I just wouldn't sleep. So I was walking around, a lot of days ... more or less in the state of a zombie." He remembers being up at all hours, perhaps sleeping for two or three hours but then lacking the ability to get back to sleep. Now, with stable tenure-track positions for both his wife and him, things have changed. He sleeps most nights now, he says, feels healthier, and "a little bit more sane most of the time."

Dr. Ampofo at Public Comprehensive openly talks about sacrifices derived from the fact that he and his wife want "the best that we can for both worlds, with our marriage and with our careers. What that means is that there are certain sacrifices that we have to make." One of them is his 45-minute commute to work because he is part of a dual-career relationship, and, as his wife commutes also, they face the scary consequence of not being able to get to their children quickly, should the necessity arise.

Having children and wanting to provide them with a family where one parent stays at home also entails sacrifices. At Community College, Dr. Thomas mentions "eating rice and beans" as a consequence of his and his wife's decision to live off one salary to enable her to stay home with the children. He describes the couple's financial conservatism and their "scrimping and saving." But they have learned to be tight on their budget and make it work. "Because of that, I'm here a lot," he says. "I teach overloads, and I teach all summer, and I try to do [extra work] as much as I can." There is a one-week break right between the spring and the summer semester, he says, and the college has to pay someone from each school to be on-campus to advise students. "So who wants to do that?" he asks. "Probably the guy who has hungry children, you know."

Though Dr. Thomas and his wife decided it was best for her to stay home with their children, Dr. Trenton at Private Comprehensive wishes he could do that himself, but there are no leave policies at his university that would allow such an arrangement. Father of a two-month-old daughter, he calls his administration's understanding of family-work issues "bad. There's no established leave, parental leave policy for men. . . . There's nothing institutionally; you're pretty much left on your own," he says. His only option to spend more time with his newborn would be to take leave without pay, something he does not consider viable. The alternative is research leave and getting his own funding, but "then you're under pressure to produce stuff. . . . Everyone at this institution knew we were having a baby. No one ever approached me at any time from the dean or anyone else saying 'Hey, what are you going to do about this?' If I had wanted to do something, it would have been me going up and making a little bit of a stink." He tells the story of his friend at the same institution whose wife also had a baby recently and who, after researching his leave options, reached the same conclusion: "There's just too many obstacles to do it."

Many of the participants, then, do not see the academic world as being one that fosters a balance between the personal and the professional given that academic work can be all-consuming if one allows it to be. In fact, Professor Sneed of Public Comprehensive, discussing his ability to balance, says, "I think the balance is in spite of the academic world. I think the academic world is about academics, and says to hell with anything else." He elaborates: "I think for male faculty, because of the way we are sort of indoctrinated, it's all about the job, and then I think we get to the job, and it's really all about the job. And at some point, the vast majority of people are going to say that the job is too much, and then they quit, or they retire in place, and both of those preclude creating knowledge. I'm not sure which one is actually even worse."

Professor Ashcroft of HBCU shares his assessment and says that the work starts to "mushroom, and without me really realizing it, I think it was taking up more time than I needed to give." Professor McDaniels of Community College sums it up this way: "There's never enough time. There are never enough hours in the day, you know." This idea is echoed by midcareer Professor Hanson of Public Comprehensive. Talking about keeping an active research agenda, he says, "it can be done, it's just very difficult; it's very difficult. The demands on one's time when one is very productive can be very tough to manage." And Professor Collado at HBCU has this to say: "There are trade-offs, certainly. With less time, less personal time, there are fewer opportunities just to go out to dinner or to have friendships. . . . You can't spend as much time as you want with friends or family, and with the e-mail and Internet, now of course your workplace is always with you, so it's even harder to negotiate that. . . . In terms of trying to balance, the academy, I think, in many ways is more exploitative than private business because people assume that you're doing things altruistically, and so they dump more and more things on you."

Not having enough time is not only a problem of early- and midcareer professors. Late-career Professor Eckhart at Private Comprehensive says, "I'm over here working late every day; I take work home with me at night, and we, neither I personally nor my wife and I, really get out and do nearly as much as we used to." Also in his late-career stage, Professor Riley of Flagship says he fears he is working too much. "I'm easily here by nine every morning, and I'm rarely home before 7:30."

Poor leadership translates into considerable stress for some faculty, as described by Professor Sneed at Public Comprehensive: "I think the good administrators make it obvious that they care about their faculty and try to help their faculty reach a balance, and the bad ones don't. And there are more bad ones than good ones. . . . Our dean, who I really do like as a guide, basically says well this isn't personal, and basically anything he does with anybody is, in fact personal."

Professor Selinski at HBCU believes that in terms of leadership at his institution "there have been far more hindrances than there should be. The reason is that academic standards are very, very low. They're being enforced with the sword, and so if you maintain high standards, you are under constant attack from administrators." He is of the opinion that "there is no respect for due process at all on the part of the administration." Professor Landers at Community College finds that the freedom that comes with an academic life made it difficult for him to understand the direction in which he should be moving. He says: "Well, being an academic you know that you're kind of given a lot more freedom and that kind of threw me off a lot. I went to my program head a lot and asked her can I do this or should I do this, and she'd say well, that's pretty much your decision. . . . And I'm used to telling people this is what needs to be done. . . . So that was a problem for me, getting adjusted to just how academia handles the daily routines of what to do."

Professor Jillian, a late-career faculty member at Community College, has a different take, albeit one that still creates a challenge. He comments, "The faculty has absolutely no say in anything. When I got promoted to full professor, do you know who made the decision? Human resources, not a faculty committee of my peers." In short, the participants feel that, given everything else they have to worry about, the administration should make their lives easier—however "easier" might be defined.

Regardless of career stage, many men find it challenging to create a balance because of the high expectations they encounter. Late-career Professor Rabinowitz at Public Comprehensive recounts what his career was like: "Well, there were times in my career when I simply gave up a personal life. I tell only a few people that I slept in this building more than once. . . . I slept in the female john where there used to be a cot, and I would catch a cat nap in there. There were times in my career when it was extraordinarily demanding, and I worked on short evenings and nights of sleep. So at different times, there were simply sacrifices that had to be made."

He wants it known that he harbors no resentment toward his institution and notes, "I think it was communicated to me fairly clearly what the expectations were . . . and I set about to try to meet those expectations. Did the university in any way try to soften that, or lessen the demand, or make it easier for me? Absolutely not, but I don't have any resentment."

Some faculty blame themselves for their difficulties in creating a successful life balance. As Richardson at Community College puts it, "If there's one thing, as I look back on my life, that makes me a lot more different than . . . others, is that maybe I am a little too driven . . . and I don't know if that's a bad thing or not, but it's definitely a characteristic." Professor Hanson at Private Comprehensive offers a similar response: "Part of it has to do with me taking on more stuff than I should, but in some ways, it has to be done. Somebody's got to do it, so I do it, and those are some of the limitations, I think, on finding a real balance." Professor Selinski at HBCU continues in the same vein: "It is hard to say 'no' sometimes to things that you don't need to take on, and I've had problems with that, you know, and it also is harder in a department where many people are not carrying their share of the load." Professor Thompson at Community College reinforces the idea: "I really do have, every day I have more than I can get done in a day it seems, and I've been accused of being a person who just doesn't say 'no' often enough."

In conclusion, male faculty members in this study report many costs that their careers extract and sacrifices that they are asked to make. Those run the gamut and include both the loss of relationships and the inability to forge them in the first place, or quality time with significant others. Men look back and regret their lack of attention to personal matters and important people in their lives and difficult choices they had to make between their careers and other things of central importance to them. They talk about stress and how it continues to affect, for many of them, the quality of their lives, their health, and sanity. Yet they also talk about underlying issues that may contribute to some of the challenges they face, issues of image and ego.

Image and Identity

That may be an image issue.

Many men today grapple with changing definitions of what it means to be a man. From an early age men learn to be part of what has been called "the cult of masculinity" (Pollack & Pipher, 1998). The concept entails learning appropriate scripts of operation in order to be accepted as a man. Pollack & Pipher recount the story of a telling interview with a boy who finds it difficult to cope in an academically prestigious school. His mother professes worry over his mediocre grades but he insists everything is fine. However, when the researchers question the 14-year-old, he admits, "I get a little down, but I'm very good at hiding it, it's like I wear a mask" (Pollack & Pipher, 1998, p. 4).

The authors confirm what others have said about the cultural construction of masculinity: "men in the United States . . . are taught to be masculine, which is marked by being strong, ambitious, successful, rational, emotionally controlled, aggressive, sexual, and self reliant . . . behaviors that are rewarded and naturalized" (Jandt & Hundley, 2007, p. 218). Of course, this type of thinking comes with concomitant problems. Kuefler (2001) notes, "For men, the dissonance in sex and gender is between an idealized rhetoric of masculinity, on the one hand, and the limitations and restrictions that prevent any man from realizing the ideal, on the other" (p. 3). Thus, men are forever striving toward a masculinity so idealized as to be impossible to achieve. In some cases, they are never able to reconcile what they believe society and significant others are demanding of them with what they are. Indeed, how men view themselves, their concerns about image, their ego construction, and comparisons with other professionals, are strong themes in this study.

Whereas late-career faculty usually internalized rigid role definitions, pre-tenure faculty attempt to define the nature of the roles they play rather than simply succumbing to society's definitions. As previously discussed, men are finding it necessary to take on new responsibilities at home which, for some, creates internal struggles, struggles at work, or both. Midcareer faculty either assume rather traditional views of their roles as husband and father, or they adopt new understandings about who they are at home and at work, as do some late-career men. In an attempt to tease apart how men are handling their changing realities, we will discuss ideas surrounding the male image, male privilege, comparisons with other professions, and the stress that is caused by the anticipation of retirement.

Image

How male faculty view themselves, and their concerns about the perceptions held by others, are often based on internal scripts of what it means to be a man. Some men feel they are not living up to the expectations their peers harbor for them.

Early-career Professor Williams at Private Comprehensive University, for instance, remembers how his need to work so much in the lab as a Ph.D. student created significant strain on his first marriage. In an attempt to placate his wife, he tried to come home at a certain time every evening and not work on Sundays; however, making these accommodations caused problems at work.

> The fact that I worked when I was in graduate school, every Saturday, was a huge source of strain . . . at that time I was coming home, probably at six or six-thirty at night, every night, and when I came home, I always felt guilty for coming home so early because all of my friends . . . were working until seven or eight o'clock every night. . . . There was significant peer pressure for me to stay longer. Occasionally, people would ask if I was going to come to work on Sunday to finish

something up, and I never wanted to come to work on
Sunday because I always dedicated that day as time that
I spent at home.

Clearly, he cannot please everyone. His second wife is more
understanding about his work requirements; however, he still
wishes the university defined a workday "where they said we're
going to lower our expectations for research for young professors
commensurate with we want you to work a forty-hour week."

His experiences reflect an often grueling reality, as described by
pre-tenure faculty HBCU Dr. Selinski: "I was often getting up at
4 or 5 in the morning, would work until dinner time, come home,
have dinner with the family, and then go back to work until
sometimes 12 or 2 at night, and then sleep for several hours and
go back again. . . . I supported my family throughout my Ph.D. so
that my wife did not have to work outside the home, and it was
hard on me, but it was the right decision."

Being a man, for him, meant shouldering the responsibility
to take care of his family regardless of professional expectations.
He declined a job offer because his wife did not like the location,
something he calls doing "the good family man thing." His understanding of what it meant to be a good "family man," however, led
to significant internal conflicts, and his marriage eventually failed.
When asked what drives men to work seventy hours a week, he
comments on how men are inculcated into a system of beliefs
about what being a man is all about: "I think part of the reason
is that we have the idea that we should be providers, and I think
we should. And when you have this mind-set, then, it's very, very
important that you be able to provide for your family, to provide
well for them, and you feel like a failure if you haven't done that."

Midcareer Professor Sneed at Public Comprehensive University
discusses his wife's unwillingness to tolerate his 80-hour work
weeks. Asked about facing the choice of either losing his wife and
children or cutting back on work, he displays a sense of internal

resolution: "I think that ultimately you just decide that this is the way you want to live your life. . . . I became okay with not being the absolute best."

Discussing his schedule, Professor Mahoney of Public Comprehensive University still struggles with his image of how a man is supposed to work. He says, "Still, I actually think if I was home more than one day a week I would start to feel a little bit guilty, like I'm slacking off or something. Even if I was working, I think I would still feel that way just because that's kind of the expectation that I grew up with. . . . I would almost rather come in and not get anything done, at least I'd feel like I came in."

One man in the study took a back seat to his wife's career and has learned to accept it. Professor Molina of Community College finds ways in his professional world to negotiate the male image; he believes his role as a father allows him to curtail his aspirations and to resist societal expectations. He has found a way to stay in teaching, which he enjoys, rather than succumb to pressures of "moving up" into administration. What allows him to do this is fatherhood. He says, "I'm getting a lot out of this stage in my life. . . . I use to some extent this stage in my life as a father of still pretty young children as cover for not pursuing, in my mind, too quickly a move out of what I would consider to be what I really wanted to do during my midcareer, which is teach." He also realizes that he can get away with things, such as taking his children to department meetings, which might damage a woman's reputation and make her appear weak. Yet he also knows that it is more difficult for him as a man to turn down new projects. In his words, "I think I have some problems saying 'no' as a man . . . that a female cohort . . . in my same position, let's say who had a spouse in my spouse's same position who was really the primary bread-winner [wouldn't have a problem with]. . . . That may be an image issue that I still do have a challenge with in terms of being really able to say 'no' to something." He realizes, however, that he can play academe against itself. He points out: "The . . . thing about academia that's so wonderful really is that it pretends to be very enlightened and politically correct. . . . So it has to live up to that image of itself not calling somebody on something like that [being a man and taking his kids to a meeting], but it's also, as I said earlier, in some ways we are still living according to some old scripts of how things are supposed to work."

Late-career faculty face a different set of struggles, such as accepting what they have professionally accomplished as they get closer to the end of their careers. Some consequently work more rather than less. As Professor Eckhart at Private Comprehensive University puts it: "I think it's also partially due to the fact that I'm getting close to retirement; there are some things that I haven't accomplished that I would like to accomplish before I retire, so probably it's a self-imposed burden that I'm working more. . . . It's not entirely other forces beyond my control; it's partially due to some personal needs or some needs that need to be fulfilled that I'm fulfilling."

Yet others deal with the realization that not everything worked out the way they thought it would. Professor Jackson at Flagship University voices strong regrets, primarily because he was never awarded an endowed chair, whereas those he taught managed to attain what he was never able to acquire. He notes: "My students, in review, have chairs at universities, I don't. But something was done for them." Another worry, of course, is the anticipation of retirement, an issue discussed separately later in this chapter.

Many men struggle with internal conflicts surrounding their values and beliefs of what they should be able to accomplish, and these conflicts make it difficult to balance work and family responsibilities. As Professor Sneed points out:

> I was pretty much obsessed with work to the detriment
> of family. . . . In order to do what I felt that I needed
> to do, I would really be here until 1:00 in the morn-
> ing, 2:00 in the morning, 3:00 in the morning, and that

doesn't work. It just didn't work. . . . Getting control of
my ego, I think, was a major piece of having a healthy
balance, and realizing that ultimately what I do for a
living, albeit incredibly enjoyable and fun and the thing
that I would choose to do over and over again, is not
really who I am. It's a piece.

Discussing what caused him to work so hard, he acknowledges
"the ego, the desire to be wonderful" led him to make the sacrifices he made. Professor Ashcroft of HBCU also admits that the
stress between his home and work life is, in part, attributable to
his own ego. He says, "Yes, it is, it gets into that ego thing, and
not saying 'no,' then realizing later, 'Why did I do that? I could
have said no.'"

Perhaps these dynamics are, if not unique, particularly pronounced among academics. Being used to success creates the
pressure to continue on that path and, if necessary, sacrifice one's
personal life. This notion is personified in men like Professor
Rabinowitz, who slept on the couch in the woman's restroom
rather than going home, or Professor Sneed, who came close to
losing his family. Some learn to resolve this dilemma; Professor
Sneed is an example: "I remember sitting down and thinking, I can
be the best professor in the entire world at what I do, or I can try to
be a good husband and father and be a really good professor, and so
instead of staying out all night and working. . . . I decided it really
wasn't worth it."

Male Privilege

Although most men in this study would not view their positions
as privileged, a number of factors nevertheless advantage them
in comparison with women. When late-career Professor Ingrahm
of Public Comprehensive University was asked what advice he
had for junior faculty, he gave a response that proved typical for

the participants: "I would advise people not to have kids early." Echoing this sentiment, early-career Professor Trenton of Private Comprehensive University has this to say:

> If I were a woman and I were trying to teach in the same semester that I was feeding that child, that would be really challenging, and I would probably be insistent on a leave. I would tell any of my people not to have a baby now because they couldn't get leave; it would just be impossible. . . . I was not going to delay the tenure clock or anything; I was going to keep on going. That's sort of a male privilege, so to speak, and I think a lot would depend on what their domestic partner, what the situation looked like, but you would assume that if they're married, the male would probably have a full time job and not giving it up, so there would be more pressure to cut out your own work.

The men seemed largely unaware that, because of a ticking biological clock, most women entering academe may not have the opportunity to wait until they have tenure before they have children. Asked about this problem, Professor Dotolo of Private Comprehensive responds: "I hadn't thought about that; this is an option available to men because if you wait until your late thirties early forties, and you're a woman, you should be nervous about that. . . . You run out of time." Professor Molina of Community College illustrates a burgeoning awareness. In his words, "I think a man is in a better position in the early, early years, in literally say the first twenty-four months, to be able to carry on professionally in terms of the amount of time that's required. Not an ideal position, but in a better position simply than the woman."

Some late-career faculty, in particular, lacked understanding of what it means to raise children and run a home. Professor Jillian of Community College, for example, whose wife lost her job as a molecular biologist when her facility closed, was asked what she proceeded to do, and gave the following response: "Essentially nothing. Raised two kids. I guess that keeps her busy enough." Professor Jackson of Flagship University, whose son and daughter-in-law are both academics, believes that it is not possible for them both to have productive careers and children, too. He says, "My son should hire a surrogate mother to be the substitute for the young female professional during the time of her academic novi-tiate. . . . Whatever we do to redress the balance, we do in defi-ance of the hunter-gatherer notion that the woman sits at home with the kids while the hunter goes and gathers."

This theme of rearing children being women's work sur-faced among late-career faculty. Professor Rabinowitz at Public Comprehensive explains how he has had more time to focus on his work because of his divorce. In his words, "I was divorced at the time and was no longer 50% responsible for the raising of a young person, my son, and so that produced a dramatic change in my life." Considering how important being a father is to many of the pre-tenure faculty, this notion of forgoing one's personal life in order to work seems to be fading however. Changing mind-sets concerning life-work balances, in turn, can only be expected to revolutionize how academe organizes work.

Comparisons with Other Professions

Many men in the study entered colleges and universities after having worked in industry, or they have close friends and family who have jobs outside of academe. Most of them believe they are in a much better position to balance their personal and profes-sional lives now than in their previous workplaces or than their friends and family. Professor Chambers of Private Comprehensive says about his schedule: "Those are things that allow for me to have time with people and with the family that other people just don't and, as a consequence, it seems to me that academics have a

much greater opportunity for work-life balance than other people."
Professor Eggleston at Public Comprehensive echoes the sentiment: "I feel like the fact that you have flexible scheduling and
that you can do whatever is required when you want to do it is the
biggest benefit you could have, and it dominates what a company
could do in terms of on-site day care or some of the other perks
that some companies provide. That might be an old school attitude, but that's where I come from." Professor Metzger at Flagship
University sums it up neatly: "My father's family were sharecrop-
pers . . . and very poor, but they did to their entire credit work
all the time. If they weren't working it was either because there
wasn't any work to do around that time or bad weather or something like that." According to him, no matter how hard academic
work might become, it beats sharecropping. Professor Jankovich
at Public Comprehensive University talks about the difference
between his work in industry and his current life as an academic.
"You were expected to be there 8 to 5, five days a week, and here
you're not. Here, at two o'clock, I may throw some things in my
briefcase . . . but that doesn't mean the day is over. . . . And that's
really why I like it a lot more than I did in industry."

Professor Zavella of HBCU, who had worked in the corporate
world before he entered higher education, had to find a new way
of seeing himself as a professional. He says, "I never knew I would
end up being a nurturing type of guy that educates. I always
thought I would go and keep on wearing my pinstripe suit and
put in sixty-five or seventy hours a week and travel here, travel
there." However, his academic life compares favorably with his
previous career. "I would put in so many hours, and most of the
job also entailed a lot of visits to clients and socializing with clients. When I realized that it was ten o'clock and I hit the snooze
button repeatedly and I didn't want to get out of bed, I knew that
something wasn't right." He believes his current schedule is much
more amenable to being a good father and husband. However,
there is a downside to faculty life compared to other professions.

Many participants mentioned how the academic life can subsume everything else, which seems to happen less in many other professions. Late-career Professor Metzger at Flagship University puts it this way: "I mean if somebody is a biochemist, I don't know you're going to take your biochemistry knowledge into your everyday life, but if you're in economics, that's everyday stuff, and if you're inside sociology or those kinds of things, or education, a whole lot of things where they're the stuff of everyday life, and that makes a big difference." Professor Lewis of Public Comprehensive is also aware of the strain an academic schedule can put on one's personal life. Says he: "In fact, with my own children, I encouraged them for the sake of their families to not go into academia because a 9-to-5 job is much more conducive to family life. . . . I was up at 10:30 at night removing advisors' blocks from students' accounts so they could register."

Retirement

Historically the concept of retirement is relatively new, and yet many people do retire nowadays, and often spend many years in retirement (Bee & Bjorklund, 2004, p. 262). As previously mentioned, late-career faculty in this study tend to think about retirement, and quite a few worry about how their image will be affected once they no longer work. In the words of Professor Green, a late-career faculty member at Private Comprehensive University: "They go from being a person, a somebody, in the department at the university which is their identity, to the day after retirement it's like you never existed. That's difficult . . . because for twenty-five years the university has given me a sense of identity. . . . My opinion means something, my work with my students has an effect on their lives, but as I said, the day after retirement all that stops. You need to be able to handle that. If I can manage getting by that, everything will be fine."

They devoted their entire lives to their careers, and have often done so to the detriment of personal relationships. As they begin to contemplate their lives outside of academe, concern begins to register. Professor Metzger at Flagship University recalls a conversation with a colleague in another discipline as they prepared to go to the human resources office to discuss retirement. He says: "He was a chemist, and I thought, well I can continue to do what I was doing because I don't need a lab. He has to have a lab to do what he does. I could, but at this point without support, he can't function at all in his field. On the other hand, I can do work in my field." Finding himself at the cusp of retirement, in other words, his main worry is how to continue to be productive.

The idea of continuing to work was prevalent among those in the study who discussed retirement. Professor Riley of Flagship put is this way: "I hope we have the advantage of having a relatively large amount of space here, so I'll be able to keep an office, at least for the time being, and keep the connections I have with the department." Professor Green of Private Comprehensive elucidates his fear of retirement quite eloquently:

> The only obstacle now is retirement . . . and what I see is that my next problem is knowing what I'm going to do in retirement. If I can't resolve that issue, and I've been thinking about it a lot, then I think then these good times will continue, barring poor health. . . . I need to have something to do when I retire. I need to have projects . . . other research projects and books and this kind of thing. . . . I don't want to be sitting at home the day after retirement wondering what in the hell I'm going to do. . . . Some of my colleagues . . . it's as if retirement is a death sentence for them. Now they are no longer important. Their opinion is no longer valued. That's difficult.

Since the men's identities are very much defined by their work, losing those jobs means losing their identity.

In conclusion, whether we call it a paradox of competing ideologies (Boon, 2005) or whether we call it an issue of cultural scripts (Levant & Richmond, 2007), men continue to have to learn to negotiate their lived experiences within the cultural paradigms that control masculinity. Using the idea of scripts that control men's lives provides a way of conceptualizing how the men in our study deal with the male image and ego. For ease of understanding, it helps to think of men juggling male images as a negotiation of the different scripts that control them. The first script revolves around the idea that as men, they are responsible for being successful at work regardless of what it takes. The second script revolves around their roles as fathers. Nicholas Townsend (2002), breaking men's roles down further into work, home, marriage, and children, finds that men must learn "to reconcile competing ideals, demands, and responsibilities" (p. 30).

However it is viewed, the underlying understanding is that men have a responsibility to work as hard as they possibly can in order to be successful in their careers and, increasingly, they must find ways to shoulder their responsibilities as fathers, lovers, husbands, and the myriad other roles they assume in their personal lives. This idea is not entirely new; men have been striving to work out contending roles for at least the last half of the twentieth century. As women began to expect equality in their relationships, men's ability to fulfill these new expectations began to compete with inculcated work scripts.

One of the ways in which scripts control men is by making it incumbent on them to project the image of being capable. This image stipulates that men work as much as necessary to achieve the success they believe is required of them. For many male faculty, this means obtaining tenure, and eventually, becoming a full professor. As research demands increase, faculty work harder and harder to achieve the requisite number of publications and grants required for promotion. It is no wonder that men have such a difficult time resolving how to imagine themselves, especially when they receive conflicting ideas about how to be. Peel, Caine, and Twomey (2007) believe research is necessary to figure out "What do men do with the scripts that describe and prescribe manliness? [and] How do they understand them?" (p. 248). Though some of the questions go beyond the scope of the research for this book, our findings may help clarify how male faculty negotiate these scripts.

In the past, men were able to meet their professional obligations without concerning themselves with domestic duties given their stay-at-home wives who ensured those responsibilities were met. However, there is a greater expectation to be actively engaged in raising children and shouldering a fair share of housework. Considering that their partners are working as hard as they are in their own professions, it seems only reasonable that men accept the new division of labor. Especially junior male faculty define their role as fathers as extremely important, and they want to be actively engaged parents. A problem arises from the inherent disconnect between the two scripts seeking to define their lives and daily operations. It is hardly possible to work 80 hours a week, which is what many believe defines their institutions' expectations and, simultaneously, be active fathers and fully participating partners. Thus, men struggle to reconcile these disparities. In some cases, the outcome is divorce. In other cases, men lower their career expectations, or they choose to dedicate themselves to their careers and not have children. However, role expectations do exert a strong influence on how men shape their work-life balance (Clausen, 1995).

Regardless of whether or how this struggle is ultimately resolved, the scripts shaping men's behavior tend to be in conflict. No one should have to choose between being a successful professor and being a successful father, a choice similar to the one between career and motherhood women have been asked to make for a long time. Townsend (2002) concludes on the basis of in-depth research that, in order to be happy, men need more than just a fulfilling work life. The early-career faculty members in this study see work and family absorbing their time to the extent that little time is left to spend on themselves, but they do manage for the most part to balance the "images" they have of themselves as fathers and professors. Most midcareer faculty have reached some type of resolution, but one that for many of them required life-altering changes—divorce, threat of loss of family, loss of family, and so forth. Those late-career faculty who have regrets seem to lament that they did not achieve the level of success at work they were hoping for, or they realize that their self-image is tied up with what they "do," not who they are. All in all it becomes clear that "family experiences were seen as making greater contributions than outside work to overall well-being" (Lewis, 1986, p. 14) and, given those realities, institutions of higher education are increasingly called to address the task of helping to make work and life more compatible, for everyone.

Resource A

Exemplary Institutions

In order to promote policies that enable faculty to balance work-life responsibilities, we provide this resource. We chose six institutions with characteristics similar to those that employed the faculty members we interviewed in the women's and men's studies. To facilitate the use of this resource, we have used the following organization. After a brief description of each institution, we provide URLs that link to information about policies and programs these institutions created to address work-life issues. According to interviews with faculty and administrators at each given college or university, many of the services are cost neutral. Programs for sick-child care, for instance, provide at-home care for children, and though it is run by the institutions, the cost is handled by the individual using the services. Or babysitting networks are organized linking students who wish to babysit with faculty who need a sitter. Since faculty have often moved away from their support networks, services such as these are invaluable to faculty but do not cost the institution.

The Institutions

University of Washington (UW). UW was founded in 1861, which makes it one of the oldest state-supported institutions of higher education on the West Coast. With an enrollment of over 40,000 students and an endowment of $1.6 billion, the university is internationally known for the high quality of its research and graduate programs.

University of Michigan. The University of Michigan was founded in 1817 in Detroit. It was not until 1837, however, that Ann Arbor became its official home (University of Michigan, 2010). Today UM serves over 40,000 students from all fifty states and 117 countries. According to Jeff Frumkin, assistant provost and senior director of academic human resources, UM's concern with work-life balance issues "goes back to the early 90s." Its commitment to assisting faculty in balancing their work-life responsibilities is evident in what the president believes is part of the university's mission. The president is quoted as proclaiming that "supporting our faculty as they balance their professional and personal lives is a high priority" (University of Michigan, 2005b). This attitude is echoed by Provost Sullivan who told us that the University of Michigan "wants to be an employer of choice."

University of California. As a system, the University of California offers some of the best work-life policies and benefits available in U.S. institutions of higher education. The Berkeley campus opened in 1869 in Oakland and moved to its present location in 1873. The institution was a merger of a private college in Oakland and a new land grant institution, and it serves 35,409 graduate and undergraduate students today.

Founded in 1919 as the southern branch of the University of California and presenting programs to 260 junior college students and 1,078 students in the teacher training program, the Los Angeles campus today has a total student enrollment of 37,476 undergraduate and graduate students. The policies offered by the University of California (UC) are, as professor and codirector of the Center for Economics & Family Security at the University of California, Berkeley's School of Law Mary Ann Mason put it, "the floor but not the ceiling." Each campus, in other words, can add to the system's package.

Williams College. Established in 1793, Williams has a total student enrollment of 2,185 students with thirty-three majors as well as concentrations and special programs (Williams College,

2010a). Williams' mission is to "provide the finest possible liberal arts education by nurturing in students the academic and civic virtues, and their related characteristics" (Williams College, 2010b). Williams College strives to create policies and programs to assist faculty with balancing work-life responsibilities on a scale commensurate with its size. It may, therefore, well serve as an example for other, similarly sized colleges. In an effort to make their campus more family-friendly, Dr. Alonzo (pseudonym), a longtime faculty member with knowledge of Williams' efforts in this area, tells us that "one of the things we recognized is that faculty recruitment and retention was going to be an issue for us." Therefore, Williams launched a "top-down initiative" focusing on work-life issues; the institution understands that, without this focus, recruiting and retaining the best faculty will become increasingly difficult. Although not able to provide some of the programs that larger institutions offer, Williams has addressed its faculty's work-life balance issues.

Boise State University. Boise State University is a metropolitan research university, located in Idaho's capital. Consisting of seven colleges, its undergraduate and graduate programs serve almost 20,000 students in more than 190 fields of interest (Boise State, n.d.-b). Though its formal efforts at becoming family-friendly began only a few years ago, the university has made remarkable strides in designing and implementing progressive policies and programs to serve its faculty, staff, and students.

San Bernardino Valley College. The history and organization of the community college system in California is unique. The San Bernardino Community College District (SBCCD) is one of seventy-two community college districts in California with a mission "to promote the discovery and application of knowledge, the acquisition of skills, and the development of intellect and character in a manner that prepares students to contribute effectively and ethically as citizens of a rapidly changing and increasingly technological world" (SBCCD, 2010b). Each district then contains a certain number of colleges and centers located within its boundaries, and San Bernardino Valley College (Valley College) is one of the campuses in SBCC. Dr. Jiminez (pseudonym), a faculty member at Valley College, tells us that, as far as he knows, "no issues have been brought up about work/life balance in the Faculty Senate." However, compared to the community college where we conducted the research on male and female faculty, Valley College does have at least some programs and policies in place that assist its faculty with work-life balancing. In fact, in acknowledging these issues, Dr. Jiminez notes that a lack of "spousal hire policies has been a little bit of a problem for us," an indication that community college systems, just as four-year institutions, may have to develop a growing awareness of work-life questions if they hope to recruit and retain the best faculty possible.

Resource B

Exemplary Policies

Developing policies that aid faculty with work-life balance issues takes time, and yet it is increasingly seen as a necessary investment. Therefore, in order to assist institutions who wish to progress, we have provided a list of exemplary institutions and links to their policies. The list is not exhaustive; however, we believe it provides a good starting point for policymakers who wish to help faculty in addressing issues surrounding child care, spousal/partner hiring, child leave, and tenure.

Child Care

Though all of the institutions provide on-campus day care, they realize that they will never be able to create enough spaces to accommodate everyone. Thus, they have come up with creative ways to assist faculty.

www.washington.edu/admin/hr/benefits/worklife/childcare/index.html

This site at the University of Washington provides information about all areas of child care. There is information about the child care that is available on campus as well as outside providers. In addition, the university provides links to information about sick-child care and local public schools.

www.hr.umich.edu/worklife/

At the University of Michigan's work-life resource center website, there are links that help parents find on-campus day care, and sick-child care. Like UW, Michigan has a program in place to help parents if their children are sick.

www.faculty.diversity.ucla.edu/worklife/school/index.htm

This website provides information about on-campus day care facilities, non-affiliated day care facilities in the area, and local schools.

http://berkeley.edu/work/child.shtml

This website lists university child-care programs for families of students, faculty, and staff. It also provides a link to an online guide that helps faculty and staff manage both home and work responsibilities. This online guide also links to additional resources.

http://wiki.williams.edu/display/handbooks/Child+Care;jsessionid=E46F981F6C45AC5A60F025A67CA3B9CC

This website gives information about child care both on and off campus and the babysitter network set up by Williams, which links students who want to babysit with faculty who need babysitters.

http://childrenscenter.boisestate.edu/

This website provides information about the university's nationally accredited "Children's Center." In addition, a link from the center's website suggests criteria to use when looking for child care elsewhere such as relationships, curriculum, teaching and teachers, assessment, health, and so on.

www.valleycollege.edu/Facilities/Child_Development_Center/
index.php

Valley College does provide on-campus day care. However, additional information about finding quality day care is not provided.

Spousal/Partner Hiring

Issues surrounding spousal/partner hiring create stress for faculty. For recruitment purposes, the institutions developed resources and policies that help make them attractive to potential faculty. From participation in higher education consortiums to creative ways of creating tenured positions for spouses and partners, these institutions tackle this problem in ways that make potential new faculty aware that they understand the importance of this issue.

www.provost.umich.edu/programs/dual_career/

This website provides information about Michigan's dual-career program such as dual-career hire initiatives at the university as well as the higher education consortium in which Michigan participates.

http://ucfamilyedge.berkeley.edu/initiatives.html

This website gives an overview of their initiatives and provides a link to resources available at Berkeley for faculty who come with a spouse or partner. There are links to employment assistance as well as information on other issues relevant to relocating to a new area. Berkeley also participates in the Northern California Higher Education Resource Consortium which presents job listings at academic institutions within close proximity.

www.faculty.diversity.ucla.edu/worklife/dual/index.htm

This website provides information for dual-career partners both in and out of academe.

http://wiki.williams.edu/display/handbooks/SPEC+Office;jses sionid=6E2AEC3BD5F8724BD9EE84B0EC3963EA

This website provides a number of resources for dual-career spouses and partners of Williams' faculty. Included is information pertaining to academic careers as well as nonacademic careers. The Academic Career Network "offers spouses and partners of Williams College faculty and administrative staff Web-based access to faculty, research, and administrative openings at a cluster of nearby institutions, as well as the ability to post credentials in a searchable database accessible to prospective employers at member schools" (Williams College, 2010d). The college also provides a host of services for nonacademic spouses/partners. Although no promise of employment is made, the amount of attention Williams gives this issue illustrates the relatively life-friendly culture of the institution.

www.boisestate.edu/policy/policy_docs/4240_FacultyDual-CareerProgram.pdf

This link leads to Boise State's progressive and comprehensive dual-career policy. Boise State has created a unique system that encourages dual-career hires by providing incentives for its departments to hire dual-career partners or spouses.

Child Leave

Exemplary institutions showcased in this book created policies which indicate that they understand the need for parents, both fathers and mothers, to have time to bond with and take care of newborn or adopted infants and children.

www.washington.edu/admin/hr/polproc/prostaff/leave/family .html

This website outlines the University of Washington's parental leave policies which go beyond the provisions we found at any of the institutions where we interviewed faculty members. A female faculty member at UW who gives birth is covered under the sick leave policy and thus eligible for ninety days of paid leave. Her salary continues for that time period during which she is usually on the payroll. The woman must provide written certification from a health care provider, attesting to the fact that she is unable to work because of her pregnancy, childbirth, or recovery. Up to four months of parental leave may be granted to an employee with a natural newborn, adoptive, or foster child. Parental leave must be taken during the first year after the child's birth or placement and does not extend beyond four months. The employee's supervisor may approve additional parental leave.

http://hr.umich.edu/worklife/leaves/index.html

This website provides links to parental leave policies at the University of Michigan. Understanding that the birth or adoption of a child is a major life event, Michigan has some of the most forward-thinking policies available. New child leave at Michigan provides the new parent with one semester off. If both parents work for the university, each parent receives a semester of childcare leave. Michigan's policy provides considerable support for families and enables them to adjust to this major life event. In addition to taking leave, faculty have the opportunity to modify teaching assignments and have a reduced load for two semesters rather than taking one full semester off. This flexibility provides faculty with a number of options so that they can create the schedule that is most workable for them and their families. This institution's policies for child leave not only go above and beyond any of the institutions covered by our interview studies, they go above and beyond many of the other exemplary institutions we researched. In fact, we would argue that their policy on child leave could be a model for other institutions in the country.

www.ucop.edu/acadadv/family/leaves.html#childbearing

http://ucfamilyedge.berkeley.edu/initiatives.html

The first website provides information about the University of California's parental leave policies. The second website provides information that is specific to the Berkeley campus. The maternity/paternity leave policies offered by the UC system provide time for both parents to learn to accommodate a child into their lives. Faculty also may take advantage of an available short-term disability policy in order for a total amount of leave of four months. In addition, the UC system has created a program for new parents called Active Service Modified Duties, which is explained on the websites. What these policies actually mean, according to UC Berkeley administrator Dr. Mary Ann Mason, is "two semesters off for new mothers and one semester for dads" (personal communication). Therefore, new mothers are provided time during their children's first year to grow accustomed to having a new baby. It also indicates an understanding of the importance of fathers by providing them with a semester to bond and be actively engaged in their children's care. Graduate students with any kind of graduate assistantship are granted up to six weeks of paid child leave.

http://wiki.williams.edu/display/handbooks/FMLA

This website provides information on Williams' family and parental leave policies, which are quite progressive. Faculty "have the option of being released from all or part of their teaching duties in the semester during or following the birth of a child. . . . The faculty member may elect either a one-semester maternity leave at 3/4 pay or the equivalent of a one-course reduction without loss of pay for the semester following childbirth. The faculty member will normally elect to combine this maternity leave with a paid parental leave, for a total of one semester's leave at full pay." As a result, any new parent can receive a one-course teaching load reduction for a semester, which is in essence a 50 percent reduction in teaching responsibilities because faculty at Williams have a 2/2 load. Inherent in the policy is the acknowledgment that new fathers need time to adjust to their role just as new mothers do. So, new parents, not just the biological mother, have the opportunity to take a semester off with 3/4 pay.

www2.boisestate.edu/pres/pres%20Cab/materialsOct2006.pdf

This link gives information about Boise State's flexible workload program. Though not specifically targeted at child leave, it does provide enough flexibility to assist new parents. Leave resulting from pregnancy, childbirth, or adoption of a child is covered by one of the less progressive policies at Boise State given that it provides little more than the Family and Medical Leave Act. However, as emphasized by Provost Andrews, Boise State's career flexibility policies, especially its flexible workload program, "provide somewhat of a safety net for the lack of generosity on the maternity policy side" (personal communication). Specifically, the flexible workload (also known as differentiated load) policy allows tenured and tenure-track faculty flexibility in how they allocate their time in regard to research, teaching, and service. They are able to shift, for example, all teaching requirements to one semester so that they are free to pursue their research or special opportunities that may arise during the next semester. It also means that during the semester when the faculty member does not teach, he or she does not physically have to be on campus and is therefore free to engage in special care duties for a child, family member, aging parent, and so on.

www.sbccd.org/Include/HR%20%20Documents/CTA%202007_2010%20Agreement.pdf

This link provides an explanation of the rules established in a bargaining agreement for the faculty at community colleges in California. The document provides information about parental leave for faculty. The bargaining agreement under which they operate provides ten days of sick leave each year they work, and it accrues. Another important benefit is called Extended Sick Leave, which is good for up to five months of leave, or one academic semester. Thus, there is flexibility in the policy so that faculty, male or female, who need time to care for a new child, may have it.

Tenure

Though most institutions offer a stoppage of the tenure clock for one year due to the birth of a child, the exemplary institutions provide more flexibility. In the case of Berkeley, the stoppage of the tenure clock is automatic, so there is no perceived bias for faculty. Only institutions who make adjustments or modifications of this one-year stoppage policy are listed.

www.washington.edu/admin/acadpers/prospective_new/ffp.html

This website outlines UW's policies in terms of tenure extensions and modifications. For one, UW offers its faculty stopping of the tenure clock. Beyond that, a faculty member at UW can decide to choose among several part-time tenure-track options. Specifically, he or she may be initially appointed for the duration of three years at 50 percent or greater of full-time responsibilities. If the appointment is renewed, the second appointment allows the faculty member to choose to work at 90 percent or more of the full-time load for three years, 70–89 percent for four years, 60–69 percent for five years, or 50–59 percent for the duration of six years. At the end of the second probationary period, whatever its length, the faculty member will be reviewed for tenure and promotion. Provided it is in the written agreement by the dean of the assistant professor's school or college, the faculty member may, at any time, change the percentage and terms of the appointment, as long as they are consistent with the numbers just mentioned.

http://spg.umich.edu/pdf/201.92.pdf

This link provides the Standard Practice Guide at the University of Michigan. Michigan does allow for a stoppage of the tenure clock. This option is available to a faculty member who must help meet the demands of caring for dependents as well as the faculty member who gives birth.

http://ucfamilyedge.berkeley.edu/initiatives.html

The website provides Berkeley's policies surrounding stopping tenure. Though all UC campuses allow for stopping the tenure clock and have an eight-year probationary period, Dr. Mason points out that on the Berkeley campus stopping the tenure clock is a default option. Faculty automatically get the tenure clock stopped unless they opt out. The benefit of this "default" option is that a faculty member has to ask *not* to stop the clock rather than to stop it; therefore, no one is made to feel as if he or she is the beneficiary of a special accommodation.

www.sbccd.org/Include/HR%20%20Documents/CTA%202007_2010%20Agreement.pdf

This link provides information pertinent to the evaluation of faculty at community colleges in California. Under the evaluation procedures, information about stopping the tenure clock is provided. The CTA Bargaining Agreement requires faculty to be evaluated "during the fall semester of the fourth year of service" (San Bernardino Community College District, 2010a, p. 54). Though the agreement does not specifically spell out that the tenure clock can be stopped, faculty member Dr. Jiminez explains that "tenure is granted after the successful completion of four fall evaluation cycles. If, for some reason, you were off for the entire fall or spring, it would mean that you have another year" (personal communication). Therefore, even though faculty's tenure would be delayed for one year if they took time off, there are no penalties for doing so.

Resource C

Key Organizations, Readings, and Websites

The following websites and readings are intended to provide a resource for those interested in implementing or researching policies that help faculty balance their work-life responsibilities. Although many of the sites and readings listed are included in the reference section, this list provides a more comprehensive resource.

Organizations and Websites

The Center for Work and Family at Boston College

www.bc.edu/centers/cwf

Sponsored by the School of Management, this website provides links to services and other resources for their university, including a link for a brochure about their services and partnerships.

Tomorrow's Professor Mailing List

http://ctl.stanford.edu/Tomprof/index.shtml

This website provides a link to articles pertinent for those planning to enter the professoriate. There is also a listserv available to those who wish to subscribe.

Alfred P. Sloan Foundation: Faculty Career Flexibility in the Academy Grants

www.sloan.org/program/32

This address is a link to the Sloan Foundation grant initiative's page. The website give a brief synopsis of the work on faculty career flexibility that the Foundation has done in partnership with the American Council on Education. There are also links to reports relevant to work-life issues.

College and University Work/Family Association

www.cuwfa.org/

This Web address is the home page of the association. It provides information about the organization's mission, events they are holding, and contact information.

Alliance for Work-Life Progress

www.awlp.org/awlp/home/html/homepage.jsp

Though not specifically geared at academe, the website has links to resources, a blog on work-life issues, and events. This site may be a good place for administrators who want to see what is going on within other industries.

National Clearinghouse on Academic Work/Life (University of Michigan Center for the Education of Women)

www.academicworklife.org/

This website creates a single place where resources are brought together. There are a number of related links that give an exhaustive list of associations and organizations, research centers and foundations, and publications.

Pennsylvania State University's The Faculty & Families Project

http://lser.la.psu.edu/workfam/facultyfamilies.htm

This website provides links to the executive summary and final report on the project and to background papers on the project.

American Association of University Professors' Resources on Balancing Family & Academic Work

www.aaup.org/AAUP/issues/WF/resources.htm

This website provides the AAUP's policy statement on Family Responsibilities and Academic Work and Web resources and articles relevant to the issue.

Further Readings

American Council on Education. (2005). *An agenda for excellence: Creating flexibility in tenure-track faculty careers.* Washington, DC: Author. Retrieved from www.acenet.edu/bookstore/pdf/2005_tenure_flex_summary.pdf.

Arreola, R. A., Theall, M., & Aleamoni, L. M. (2003). *Beyond scholarship: Recognizing the multiple roles of the professoriate.* Paper presented at the AERA Convention, Chicago. Retrieved from www.cedanet.com/meta/ Beyond%20Scholarship.pdf.

Drago, R., Colbeck, C. L., Stauffer, K. D., Pirretti, A., Burkum, K., Faziolo, J., et al. (2006, May). The avoidance bias against caregiving: The case of academic faculty. *American Behavioral Scientist, 49*(9), 1222–1247.

Gappa, J. M., Austin, A. E., & Trice, A. G. (2006). *Rethinking faculty work: Higher education's strategic imperative.* San Francisco: Jossey-Bass.

Huber, M. T. (2004). *Balancing acts: The scholarship of teaching and learning in academic careers.* Washington, DC: American Association for Higher Education and the Carnegie Foundation for the Advancement of Teaching.

Huber, M. T., & Hutchings, P. (2005). *The advancement of learning: Building the teaching commons.* San Francisco: Jossey-Bass.

Jenkins, A., & Healey, M. (2005). *Institutional strategies to link teaching and research.* York, UK: The Higher Education Academy.

Leslie, D. W. (Ed.). (1998). *New directions for higher education: No. 104. The growing use of part-time faculty: Understanding causes and effects.* San Francisco: Jossey Bass.

Leslie, D. W. (2002, January–February). Resolving the dispute: Teaching is academe's core value. *Journal of Higher Education, 73*(1), 49–73.

Marincovich, M. (2007). Teaching and learning in a research-intensive university. In R. P. Perry & J. C. Smart (Eds.), *The scholarship of teaching and learning in higher education: An evidence-based perspective* (pp. 23–38). Dordrecht, Netherlands: Springer.

Mason, M. A., & Goulden, M. (2002). Do babies matter? The effect of family formation on the lifelong careers of academic men and women. *Academe, 88*(6), 21–27.

Mason, M. A., & Goulden, M. (2004). Do babies matter (Part II)? Closing the baby gap. *Academe, 90*(6), 3–7.

Reis, R. M. (1997). *Tomorrow's professor: Preparing for academic careers in science and engineering.* Piscataway, NJ: IEEE Press.

Rice, R. E., & Sorcinelli, M. D. (2002). Can the tenure process be improved? In R. P. Chait (Ed.), *The questions of tenure* (pp. 101–124). Cambridge, MA: Harvard University Press.

Rice, R. E., Sorcinelli, M. D., & Austin, A. E. (2000). *Heeding new voices: Academic careers for a new generation.* Washington, DC: American Association for Higher Education.

Schuster, J. H., & Finklestein, M. J. (2006). *The American faculty: The restructuring of academic work and careers.* Baltimore: Johns Hopkins University Press.

Sorcinelli, M. D., Austin, A. E., Eddy, P. L., & Beach, A. L. (2006). *Creating the future of faculty development: Learning from the past, understanding the present.* Bolton, MA: Anker.

Williams, J. C. (1999). *Unbending gender: Why family and work conflict and what to do about it.* New York: Oxford University Press.

Williams, J. C. (2005, February 7). Are your parental-leave policies legal? *Chronicle of Higher Education*. Retrieved from http://chronicle.com/article/Are-Your-Parental-Leave-Pol/45098/.

Wulff, D. H., & Austin, A. E. (2004). *Paths to the professoriate: Strategies for enriching the preparation of future faculty.* San Francisco: Jossey-Bass.

References

Almqvist, A. L. (2008, Spring). Why most Swedish fathers and few French fathers use paid parental leave: An exploratory qualitative study of parents. *Fathering: A Journal of Theory, Research, and Practice About Men as Fathers*, 6(2), 192–200.

Astin, H. S., & Milem, J. F. (1997). The status of academic couples in U.S. institutions. In M. A. Ferber & J. W. Loeb (Eds.), *Academic couples: Problems and promises* (pp. 128–155). Urbana: University of Illinois.

Austin, A. E. (2002, January/February). Preparing the next generation of faculty: Graduate school as socialization to the academic career. *Journal of Higher Education*, 73(1), 94–122.

Austin, A. E. (2006). Foreword. In S. J. Bracken, J. K. Allen, & D. R. Dean (Eds.), *The balancing act: Gendered perspectives in faculty roles and work lives* (pp. ix–xiv). Sterling, VA: Stylus.

Babbie, E. (1983). *The practice of social research* (3rd ed.). Belmont, CA: Wadsworth.

Bee, H. L., & Bjorklund, B. R. (2004). *The journey of adulthood* (5th ed.). Upper Saddle River, NJ: Pearson/Prentice Hall.

Bloom, L. (2005). The two-thousand mile commute. In R. Bassett (Ed.), *Parenting and professing* (pp. 151–160). Nashville, TN: Vanderbilt University Press.

Boise State University. (n.d.-a). *Children's center*. Retrieved from http://childrenscenter.boisestate.edu/.

Boise State University. (n.d.-b). *Future students*. Retrieved from www.boisestate.edu/future/.

Boise State University. (2005). *Faculty dual-career program*. Retrieved from www.boisestate.edu/policy/policy_docs/4240_FacultyDual-CareerProgram.pdf.

Boise State University. (2009). *Faculty tenure procedures*. Retrieved from www.boisestate.edu/policy/policy_docs/4370_FacultyTenureProcedures.pdf.

Bookman, A. (2004). *Starting in our backyard*. London: Routledge.

Boon, K. A. (2005). Heroes, metanarratives, and the paradox of masculinity in contemporary western culture. *Journal of Men's Studies, 13*(3), 301–312.

Chang, C. (1999, Spring). Marginalized masculinities and hegemonic masculinity: An introduction. *Journal of Men's Studies, 7*(3), 295–314.

Clark, R. L., & d'Ambrosio, M. B. (2005). Recruitment, retention, and retirement: Compensation and employment policies for higher education. *Educational Gerontology, 31*, 285–403.

Clausen, J. A. (1995). Gender, contexts, and turning points in adults' lives. In P. Moen, G. Elder, & K. Luscher (Eds.), *Examining lives in context* (pp. 365–395). Washington, DC: American Psychological Association Press.

Colbeck, C. (2006). How female and male faculty with families manage work and personal roles. In S. J. Bracken, J. K. Allen, & D. R. Dean (Eds.), *The balancing act: Gendered perspectives in faculty roles and work lives* (pp. 31–72). Sterling, VA: Stylus.

Coley, R. B. (2001, September). Emerging research on low-income, unmarried, and minority fathers. *American Psychologist, 56*(9), 743–753.

Connell, R. W. (2003, Spring). Masculinities, change, and conflict in global society: Thinking about the future of men's studies. *Journal of Men's Studies, 11*(3), 249–267.

Drago, R., & Colbeck, C. L. (2003). *The mapping project: Exploring the terrain of U.S. colleges and universities for faculty and families.* Retrieved from http://lser.la.psu.edu/workfam/mappingproject.htm.

Ferber, M. A., & Loeb, J. W. (1997). Introduction. In M. A. Ferber & J. W. Loeb (Eds.), *Academic couples: Problems and promises* (pp. 1–24). Chicago: University of Illinois Press.

Finkelstein, M. J., Seal, R. K., & Schuster, J. H. (1998). *The new generation: A profession in transformation.* Baltimore: Johns Hopkins University Press.

Fleig-Palmer, J. M., Murin, J., Palmer, D. K., & Rathert, C. (2003). Meeting the needs of dual-career couples in academia. *CUPA-HR Journal, 54*(3), 12–15.

Gappa, J. M., Austin, A. E., & Trice, A. G. (2007). *Rethinking faculty work: Higher education's strategic imperative.* San Francisco: Jossey-Bass.

Glazer-Raymo, J. (1999). *Shattering the myths: Women in academe.* Baltimore: Johns Hopkins University Press.

Gornick, J. C., & Meyers, M. K. (2005). Supporting a dual-earner/dual-career society. In J. Heyman & C. Beem (Eds.), *Unfinished work: Building equality and democracy in an era of working families* (pp. 371–408). New York: The New Press.

Hartmann, H. (2004). Policy alternatives for solving work-family conflict. In J. Jacobs & J. F. Madden (Eds.), *Mommies and daddies on the fast track: Success of parents in demanding professions* (pp. 226–231). Thousand Oaks, CA: Sage.

Healy, C. (n.d.). *A business perspective on workplace flexibility: When work works, an employer strategy for the 21st century.* Quoted in Gappa, J. M., Austin, A. E., & Trice, A. G. (2007). *Rethinking faculty work: Higher education's strategic imperative.* San Francisco: Jossey-Bass.

Hertz, R. (2004). Working to place family at the center of life: Dual-earner and single-parent strategies. In L. Richardson, V. Taylor, & N. Whittier (Eds.), *Feminist frontiers* (6th ed., pp. 250–259). New York: McGraw-Hill.

Hesse-Biber, S. N. (2007). Feminist research: Exploring the interconnections of epistemology, methodology, and method. In S. N. Hesse-Biber (Ed.), *Handbook of feminist research: Theory and praxis* (pp. 1–28). Thousand Oaks, CA: Sage.

Higgins, C., Duxbury, L., & Lee, C. (1994, April). Impact on life-cycle stage and gender on the ability to balance work and family responsibilities. *Family Relations, 43*(2), 144–150.

Hochschild, A. (2001). The second shift: Employed women are putting in another day of work at home. In M. Kimmel & M. Messner (Eds.), *Men's lives* (pp. 439–442). Boston: Allyn & Bacon. Excerpt from *The second shift* by A. Hochschild & A. Machung (1989). New York: Viking Penguin Press.

Jacobs, J. A., & Gerson, K. (2001). Overworked individuals or overworked families? Explaining trends in work, leisure, and family time. *Work and Occupations, 28*(1), 40–63.

Jacobs, J. A., & Winslow, S. E. (2004, August). The academic life course, time pressures and gender inequality. *Community, Work & Family, 7*(2), 143–161.

Jandt, F., & Hundley, H. (2007). Intercultural dimensions of communicating masculinities. *Journal of Men's Studies, 15*(2), 216–231.

Jaschick, S. (2009). Ignorance about "stop the clock" policies. *Inside Higher Ed.* Retrieved from www.insidehighered.com/news/2009/01/06/stc.

Jones, K. B. (2005). Boomerangst. In R. Hile Bassett (Ed.), *Parenting and professing: Balancing family work within an academic career* (pp. 173–181). Nashville, TN: Vanderbilt University Press.

Klinth, R. (2008, Winter). The best of both worlds? Fatherhood and gender equality in Swedish paternity leave campaigns, 1976–2006. *Fathering: A Journal of Theory, Research, and Practice About Men as Fathers, 6*(1), 20–38.

Kramer, L. (2005). *The sociology of gender: A brief introduction* (2nd ed.). Los Angeles: Roxbury.

Kuefler, M. (2001). *The manly eunuch: Masculinity, gender ambiguity, and Christian ideology in late antiquity.* Chicago: University of Chicago Press.

Letherby, G., Marchbank, J., Ramsay, K., & Shiels, J. (2005). Mothers and "others" providing care within and outside the academy. In R. Hile Bassett (Ed.),

Parenting and professing: Balancing family work within an academic career (pp. 204–216). Nashville, TN: Vanderbilt University Press.

Levant, R. F., & Richmond, K. (2007). A review of research on masculinity ideologies using the male role norms inventory. *Journal of Men's Studies, 15*(2), 130–146.

Lewis, R. A. (1986). Introduction: What men get out of marriage and parenthood. In R. A. Lewis & R. E. Salt (Eds.), *Men in families* (pp. 11–26). Beverly Hills, CA: Sage.

Mason, M. A. (2009, February 24). Balancing act: Men and mothering. *Chronicle of Higher Education.* Retrieved from http://chronicle.com/jobs/news/2009/02/2009022401c.htm.

Mason, M. A., & Goulden, M. (2002, November/December). Do babies matter? The effect of family formation on the lifelong careers of academic men and women. *Academe Online.* Retrieved from www.aaup.org/AAUP/pubsres/academe/2002/ND/Feat/Maso.htm.

Mason, M. A., & Goulden, M. (2004). Do babies matter? (Part II) Closing the baby gap. *Academe, 90*(6), 11–16.

Mason, M. A., Goulden, M., & Frasch, K. (2009, January–February). Why graduate students reject the fast track. *Academe Online.* Retrieved from www.aaup.org/AAUP/pubsres/academe/2009/JF/feat/maso.htm.

Mason, M. A., Goulden, M., & Wolfinger, N. (2006). Babies matter. In S. J. Bracken, J. K. Allen, & D. R. Dean (Eds.), *The balancing act: Gendered perspectives in faculty roles and work lives* (pp. 9–29). Sterling, VA: Stylus.

McIntosh, P. (2000). White privilege and male privilege: A personal account of coming to see correspondences through work in women's studies. In T. Ore (Ed.), *The social construction of difference and inequality* (pp. 475–485). Mountain View, CA: Mayfield.

Milkie, M., & Peltola, P. (1999, May). Playing all the roles: Gender and the work-family balancing act. *Journal of Marriage and Family, 61*(2), 476–490.

Miller-Loessi, K., & Henderson, D. (1997). Changes in American society: The context for academic couples. In M. A. Ferber & J. W. Loeb (Eds.), *Academic couples: Problems and promises* (pp. 25–43). Chicago: University of Illinois Press.

Newberger, E. (1999). *The men they will become: The nature and nurture of male character*. Reading, MA: Perseus Books.

Noddings, N. (2003). *Happiness and education*. New York: Cambridge University Press.

Norrell, J. E., & Norrell, T. H. (1996). Faculty and family policies in higher education. *Journal of Family Issues, 17*(2), 204–226.

Olsen, D., & Sorcinelli, M. D. (1992, Summer). The pretenure years: A longitudinal perspective. In M. D. Sorcinelli & A. E. Austin (Eds.), *New directions for teaching and learning: No. 50. Developing new and junior faculty* (pp. 15–25). San Francisco: Jossey-Bass.

O'Meara, K., Terosky, A., & Neumann, A. (2008). *Faculty careers and work lives: A professional growth perspective* (ASHE-ERIC Higher Education Report). San Francisco: Jossey-Bass.

Orenstein, P. (2000). *Flux: Women on sex, work, love, kids and life in a half-changed world*. New York: Doubleday.

Palkovitz, R., Copes, M., & Woolfolk, T. (2001). "It's like . . . you discover a sense of being": Involved fathering as an evoker of adult development. *Men and Masculinities, 4*, 49–69.

Peel, M., Caine, B., & Twomey, C. (2007). Masculinity, emotion and subjectivity: Introduction. *Journal of Men's Studies, 15*(3), 247–250.

Philipsen, M. I. (2008). *Challenges of the faculty career for women: Success and sacrifice*. San Francisco: Jossey-Bass.

Pollack, W., & Pipher, M. (1998). *Real boys: Rescuing our sons from the myths of boyhood*. New York: Henry Holt.

Quinn, K., & Shapiro, R. (2009). Balance@UW: Work-family cultural change at the University of Washington. In J. Lester & M. Sallee (Eds.), *Establishing the family-friendly campus: Models for effective practice* (pp. 37–52). Sterling, VA: Stylus.

Rice, R. E., Sorcinelli, M. D., & Austin, A. E. (2000). *Heeding new voices: Academic careers for a new generation*. Washington, DC: American Association for Higher Education.

San Bernardino Community College District. (2010a). *2007–2010 CTA agreement*. Retrieved from www.sbccd.org/~/media/9CA660D92C26430DBA32AA50D1C14070.pdf.

San Bernardino Community College District. (2010b). *Welcome to the San Bernardino Community College district!* Retrieved from www.sbccd.org/pages/109.asp.

San Bernardino Valley College. (n.d.). *Child development center*. Retrieved from www.valleycollege.edu/Facilities/Child_Development_Center/index.php.

Schacht, S. (2004). Teaching about being an oppressor: Some personal and political considerations. In L. Richardson, V. Taylor, & N. Whittier (Eds.), *Feminist frontiers* (6th ed., pp. 24–29). New York: McGraw-Hill.

Schuster, J., & Finkelstein, M. (2006). *The American faculty: The restructuring of academic work and careers*. Baltimore: Johns Hopkins University Press.

Schwalbe, M., & Wolkomir, M. (2003). Interviewing men. In J. Holstein & J. Gubrium (Eds.), *Inside interviewing: New lenses, new concerns* (pp. 55–71). Thousand Oaks, CA: Sage.

Seidman, I. (2006). *Interviewing as qualitative research* (3rd ed.). New York: Teachers College Press.

Sorcinelli, M. D., & Near, J. P. (1989, January/February). Relations between work and life away from work among university faculty. *Journal of Higher Education, 60*(1), 59–81.

Spalter-Roth, R., & Erskine, W. (2005, November/December). Beyond the fear factor: Work/family policies in academia—Resources or rewards? *Change, 37*(6), 19–25.

Stanley, T. L. (2005). The one with the baby: Single-mothering in academia. In R. Hile Bassett (Ed.), *Parenting and professing: Balancing family work within an academic career* (pp. 82–88). Nashville, TN: Vanderbilt University Press.

Sullivan, B., Hollenshead, C., & Smith, G. (2004). Developing and implementing work-family policies for faculty. *Academe*, 90(6), 24–27.

Townsend, N. W. (2002). *The package deal: Marriage, work and fatherhood in men's lives*. Philadelphia: Temple University Press.

Trower, C. (2005, Fall). Gen X meets theory X: What new scholars want. *The Department Chair*, 16(2), 16–18.

University of California. (n.d.). *Family friendly policies for faculty and other academic appointees*. Retrieved from www.ucop.edu/acadadv/family/leaves.html.

University of California. (2002). *UC Berkeley's guide to work and family*. Retrieved from http://workandfamily.chance.berkeley.edu.

University of California. (2003a). *Report on the University of California: President's summit on faculty gender equity*. Retrieved from www.ucop.edu/pressummit/report.pdf.

University of California. (2003b). *The UC faculty family friendly edge: Chairs and deans toolkit*. Retrieved from http://ucfamilyedge.berkeley.edu/toolkit.html.

University of California. (2003c). *The UC faculty family friendly edge: Existing elements of the family friendly package for UC ladder-rank faculty*. Retrieved from http://ucfamilyedge.berkeley.edu/initiatives.html.

University of California. (2004). *Mission statement*. Retrieved from www.universityofcalifornia.edu/aboutuc/missionstatement.html.

University of California. (2008a). *UCLA—Campus services*. Retrieved from http://map.ais.ucla.edu/portal/site/UCLA/menuitem.

University of California. (2008b). *UCLA faculty diversity and development: Dual academic career*. Retrieved from www.faculty.diversity.ucla.edu/worklife/dual/index.htm.

University of Michigan. (n.d.-a). *Early childhood programs*. Retrieved from www.hr.umich.edu/childcare/index.html.

University of Michigan. (n.d.-b). *Work/life resource center*. Retrieved from www.hr.umich.edu/worklife/index.php.

University of Michigan. (2005a). *Childbirth and adoption*. Retrieved from www.provost.umich.edu/faculty/family/childbirth/index.html.

University of Michigan. (2005b). *Our mission*. Retrieved from www.provost.umich.edu/faculty/family/mission/index.html.

University of Michigan. (2007). *Office of the provost*. Retrieved from www.provost.umich.edu/programs/dual_career/.

University of Michigan. (2010). *University of Michigan history*. Retrieved from http://bentley.umich.edu/research/um/history.php.

University of Washington. (n.d.-a). *Academic human resources: Family friendly policies*. Retrieved from www.washington.edu/admin/acadpers/prospective_new/ffp.html.

University of Washington. (n.d.-b). *Academic human resources: Medical and family leaves*. Retrieved from www.washington.edu/admin/acadpers/faculty/medical_leave.html.

University of Washington. (2002). *Faculty handbook: Appointment and promotion of faculty members: Section 24–45. Appointment of part-time professors*. Retrieved from www.washington.edu/faculty/facsenate/handbook/02–02–24.html.

Voydanoff, P. (2005, December). The effects of community demands, resources, and strategies on the nature and consequences of the work-family interface: An agenda for future research. *Family Relations, 54*(5), 583–595.

Vygotsky, L. (1987). *Thought and language* (A. Kozulin, Ed.). Cambridge, MA: MIT Press, 236–237; cited in Seidman, I. (2006). *Interviewing as qualitative research* (3rd ed.). New York: Teachers College Press, p. 7.

Ward, K., & Wolf-Wendel, L. (2004). Fear factor: How safe is it to make time for family? *Academe, 90*(6), 28–31.

Warner, J. (2005). *Perfect madness: Motherhood in the age of anxiety*. New York: Riverhead Books.

Williams, C., & Heikes, E. (1993, June). The importance of researcher's gender in the in-depth interview: Evidence from two case studies of male nurses. *Gender and Society, 7*(2), 280–291.

Williams, J. (2000). *Unbending gender: Why family and work conflict and what to do about it.* New York: Oxford University Press.

Williams College. (2009). *Personal leave faculty.* Retrieved from http://wiki.williams.edu/display/handbooks/Personal+Leave+Faculty.

Williams College. (2010a). *Fast facts.* Retrieved from www.williams.edu/home/fast_facts/.

Williams College. (2010b). *Mission and purposes.* Retrieved from www.williams.edu/home/mission/.

Williams College. (2010c). *Office of spouse/partner employment counseling.* Retrieved from http://spec.williams.edu/.

Williams College. (2010d). *Office of spouse/partner employment counseling: Academic career network.* Retrieved from http://spec.williams.edu/academic-career-network/.

Williams College. (2010e). *Williams College babysitting service.* Retrieved from www.williams.edu/resources/babysitting.

Williams College. (2010f). *Williams College children's center: Program, curriculum, and daily schedules.* Retrieved from www.williams.edu/resources/childrenscenter/program.php.

Wilson, R. (2003, December 5). How babies alter careers for academics. *Chronicle of Higher Education,* pp. A1–A8.

Wolf-Wendel, L. E., Twombly, S. B., & Rice, S. (2003). *The two-body problem: Dual-career-couple hiring policies in higher education.* Baltimore: Johns Hopkins University Press.

Woolf, V. (1929). *A room of one's own.* New York: Harcourt Brace Jovanovich.

Woolf, V. (1999). A room of one's own. In C. Lemert (Ed.), *Social theory: The multicultural and classic readings* (2nd ed., pp. 257–258). Boulder, CO: Westview Press. (Original work published 1929).

Index

Child leave: absence of paid, 52–53; exemplary policies, 188–192; recommendations, 120–121. *See also* individual institution

Childbirth: delaying, 10–11. *See also* Child leave

Child-free faculty, 89, 103–104, 178

Children's Center, Boise State University, 72, 186

Coding, of transcripts in study, 131–132

Colbeck, C., 10–11, 25, 143

Collaboration, as coping strategy, 108

College and University Work/Family Association, 196

Communication, policy: recommendations, 123–124; when faculty meets policy, 80. *See also* individual institution

Community, family-friendly, 111

Community College: child care/child leave policy at, 63–64, 91; culture at, 94; overview of, 133–134; partner/spousal hiring at, 42; technology at, 95–96, 105

Commuter couples, 40, 46, 153–154, 156, 161

Confidentiality, 130

Corporatization of the university, 3

Credibility, of present study, 131

Cult of masculinity, 166

Cultural change: recommendations, 124–126. *See also* individual institution

Cultural scripts, 166, 167, 170, 177–179

D

Differentiated load. *See* Flexible workload

Distance learning, 95

Divorce, 58, 101, 150, 151–152, 173, 178, 179

"Do Babies Matter?" study, 52

Double shift, 31, 51

Drago, R., 10–11, 25

Dual-academic-career couples, 37–43, 153–154; career limitations, 38–39; compromise, 38, 39–40; cost of programs, 49; early-career faculty, 37; logistical problems, 40; midcareer faculty, 39–40; partner/spousal hiring, 119–120; partner/spousal hiring, at exemplary institutions, 43–47; partner/spousal hiring, at traditional institutions, 42; policy meets faculty,

48–49; recommendations, 49–50; in the past, 40–41. *See also* Dual-academic-career couples, division of labor by; Dual-career couples

Dual-academic-career couples, division of labor by, 26–37; early-career men, 28–29, 36; early-career women, 29–30, 31; end-of-career men, 37; end-of-career women, 31; by gender, 26–28; generational differences, 31, 35–36; late-career men, 34–36; midcareer men, 31–34, 36–37; and negative advantage, 29–30; by personal preference, 30–31

Dual-body problem. *See* Dual-academic-career couples

Dual-career couples: nonacademic employment services, 46, 47, 49, 120, 188; rise in number of, 27. *See also* Dual-academic-career couples

E

Eccentricity credits, 97–98

Elder care, 13, 83, 112, 121

Emmert, M., 137

Empty nester, 103, 152

Erskine, W., 99

Exemplary institutions. *See* Boise State University; San Bernardino Valley College; University of California (UC); University of California at Berkeley (UCB); University of California at Los Angeles (UCLA); University of Michigan (UM); University of Washington (UW); Williams College

Expectations: of early-career faculty, 56; ill-defined, 6–7; increase during pre-tenure period, 2–6; research productivity, 3–4; scholarly productivity, 1, 3

Experience, as enabler, 96–99

Extended family, 29, 90, 102, 104, 109, 150

Extended Sick Leave program, 78, 192

F

The Faculty & Families Project, 196–197

Family care, 14–15, 73, 112. *See also* Child care; Elder care

Family formation: men, 10, 11; women, 10–11